A Valley of Kings

THE BOYNE

Five Thousand Years of History

HENRY BOYLAN

THE O'BRIEN PRESS

A VALLEY

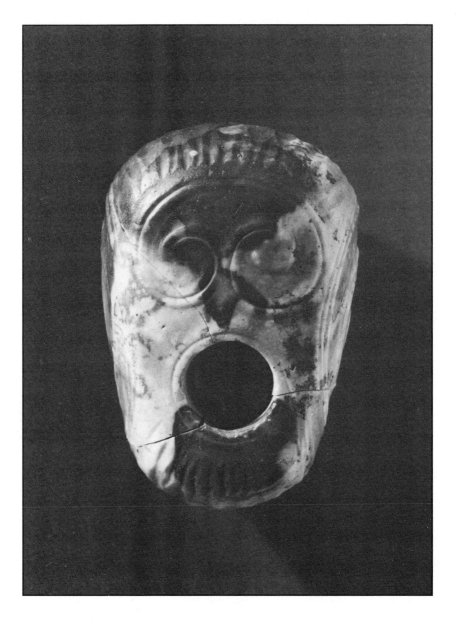

OF KINGS

The BOYNE

Henry Boylan

Five Thousand

First published in hardback 1988 by The O'Brien Press Ltd.,
20 Victoria Road, Rathgar, Dublin 6, Ireland
Reprinted 1996
Copyright © for text – Harry Boylan
Copyright © for design, layout, editing and illustrations –
The O'Brien Press Ltd.

British Library Cataloguing-in-publication Data
Boylan, Henry
Boyne: valley of Kings
1. (County) Meath, Boyne Valley, to 1987
I. Title
941.8'22

ISBN 0-86278-170-1

3   4   5   6   7   8   9   10
96   97   98   99   00   01   02   03   04   05

The O'Brien Press receives assistance from
The Arts Council/An Chomhairle Ealaíon

Cover design: Frank Murphy
Cover illustration: Office of Public Works, Dublin
Layout, design, editing: The O'Brien Press Ltd.
Printing: Colour Books Ltd.

Years of History

THE O'BRIEN PRESS • DUBLIN

Contents

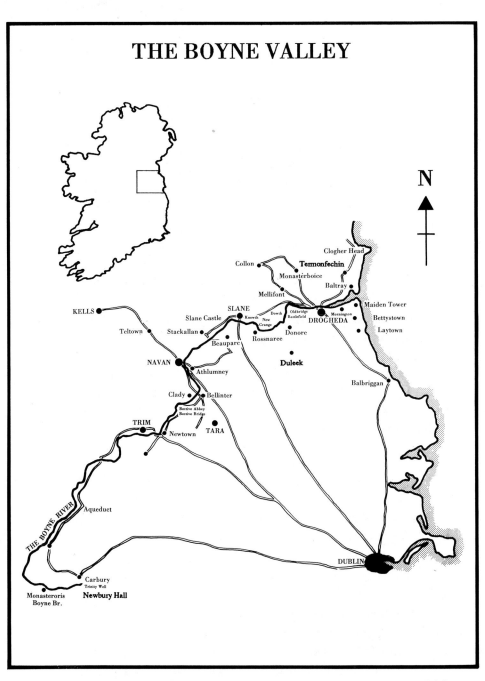

THE BOYNE VALLEY

N

Clogher Head
Collon   Termonfechin
Monasterboice
Baltray
Mellifont
Maiden Tower
KELLS   SLANE   Oldbridge
Slane Castle   Knowth Dowth Battlefield   Mornington   Bettystown
Teltown   Stackallan   New   DROGHEDA   Laytown
Grange
Beauparc   Rossnaree   Donore
NAVAN   Athlumney
Duleek
Balbriggan
Clady   Bellinter
Boctive Abbey
Boctive Bridge
TRIM   TARA
Newtown

THE BOYNE RIVER   Aqueduct

DUBLIN

Carbury
Trinity Well
Monasteroris   Newbury Hall
Boyne Br.

This map shows the course of the seventy-mile-long river Boyne from its source at Trinity Well, Carbury, County Kildare to the estuary below Drogheda. The principal places mentioned in the text are specially marked.

Introduction

'O Grandson of Conn, O Cormac, said Carbery,
What is best for a king?'
Not hard to tell,' said Cormac, 'Best for him,
Taking care of ancient lore.'
From the 'Instructions of King Cormac'

It is not by chance that the county of Meath is known as 'Royal Meath'. The most powerful kings in pre-Norman Ireland were crowned on the Hill of Tara. Two miles to the north of Tara, in a bend of the river Boyne, are the great prehistoric tombs of Newgrange, Knowth and Dowth. Many questions remain unanswered concerning these tombs and their haunting stone carvings, but one thing seems clear: such monumental constructions, on which hundreds of labourers toiled for years, were not made for the lowly, but for the mighty of the time. In his poem 'The Burial of King Cormac', Sir Samuel Ferguson echoes the tradition that Brú na Bóinne — as Newgrange is called in Irish — was a royal burial place:

In Brugh of Boyne shall be his grave,
And not in noteless Rosnaree.

Two miles downstream, seawards towards Drogheda, the Boyne sweeps round at Oldbridge in a great bend, and here in 1690 was fought the last major military engagement in Ireland, the last time two kings fought for the sovereignty of these islands.

Through this Valley of Kings flows Edmund Spenser's 'pleasant Boyne', pre-eminently Royal Meath's river, for, apart from a few miles from its source near Carbury in County Kildare, its course runs through Meath as far as famed Oldbridge, and for the remaining seven miles down to the sea it forms the boundary between Meath and Louth.

Writing in 1849 Sir William Wilde, father of Oscar, said: 'The Meathmen, who were very Irish in the last century, used to boast that they spoke better Irish and had more poets, minstrels and men of genius among them and that they were more lively and energetic than the boors of Leinster, whom they always defeated at hurling, boxing, wrestling and other athletic exercises. Up to about fifteen years ago, the men of Meath used to exhibit their powers in wrestling matches with the men of Kildare and Dublin in the Phoenix Park.'

Meath is now included in the province of Leinster, but the Meathmen of whom Sir William wrote were looking back to medieval times when Meath was part of the hegemony of the Uí Néill, rulers of the territory we now call Ulster. The Uí Néill held sway as far south as the Boyne, and south and west of it at times, for sovereignty in Gaelic Ireland fluctuated from generation to generation. If Meathmen cannot now call themselves Ulstermen, they do not care to be classed among the Leinstermen; Royal Meath stands alone.

Many battles were fought between the Uí Néill and the Leinstermen for the kingship of Tara, with only occasional and short-lived success for the Leinstermen. According to tradition, the king of Tara was the chief king in Ireland and the Uí Néill held this position for over five hundred years without serious challenge.

In its seventy miles, the Boyne flows through some of the most fertile land in Ireland. The natural wealth of the valley of the Boyne and its pastoral beauty made it prized from the beginnings of history. Its rich historical, antiquarian and literary associations make it one of the great rivers of Ireland. Whatever about the claims of the Meathmen as recorded by Sir William Wilde, the names of St. Patrick, Poynings, Oliver Cromwell, King William, Jonathan Swift, Lord Dunsany and Francis Ledwidge are reminders of the richly varied past of this valley.

Nor was it all forays and feuds. At Monasterboice there are the remains of one of the oldest monastic settlements in the country, with one of the finest high crosses extant; and Mellifont Abbey, five miles away, was the first Cistercian foundation in Ireland.

A noble river, rich woodlands and fertile pasture attracted the great and powerful to build castles and fine houses along the banks of the river. Some are now in ruins, but enough remains to bring the traveller back in time to the days of de Lacy, who built the huge castle at Trim in the twelfth century, or to a later and quieter century, when Sir Henry Tichborne built himself a beautiful house at Beaulieu, between Drogheda and the sea, which is still occupied by his descendants.

In following the course of the river from its source to the sea, one traverses good roads close to the banks and the river comes into view at many places.

In his book on the Boyne, Sir William Wilde gives an itinerary by which a Dublin resident could visit all the places of interest in three days, travelling by rail and then hiring an outside jaunting car. He counselled the traveller to take the early morning train from the Broadstone terminus of the Midland Great Western Railway to Enfield. The carman would take him to the source of the Boyne, to places of interest in the surrounding countryside and then to Moyvalley to catch the evening up-train from Mullingar. The second day the traveller should take the train to Moyvalley and then proceed by outside car to Trim and on to Navan. A branch of the Drogheda railway would take him home to Dublin. The third day would be devoted to Navan and Drogheda and the surrounding countryside. As an alternative, Sir William allowed that the traveller could proceed continuously down the river, sleeping the first night at Trim, the second at Slane and the third in Dublin, 'as neither Navan nor Drogheda as yet present the very best accommodation'.

Sir William's traveller must have been a very energetic person. Even allowing that his leisurely journey by rail would have occasioned him little fatigue, twenty or thirty miles on bad roads, jolting and swaying on an outside jaunting car, with sorties across fields to view castles and passage graves and walks around the towns of Navan and Drogheda, is a strenuous day's programme. No doubt it was much easier in those days, before motor traffic choked our towns and cities. Whatever the cause, exploration of the Boyne Valley by today's traveller in three days would be hard enough going. Besides, after some hours in that calm countryside, the very notion of timekeeping or hurry of any kind seems absurd.

To see this valley, then, and savour its astonishing wealth of history, one should traverse the course of the river from source to sea in leisurely fashion, with digressions and turnings aside, as recollections of 'old, unhappy, far-off things and battles long ago' crowd in on the memory. And that is how we proceed in the following pages, from Trinity Well at Carbury in County Kildare to the estuary at Mornington where the Boyne sweeps into the Irish Sea, watched over by the Maiden Tower.

Chapter 1

*Source - Glynn Crossroads - Trim -
Duke of Wellington - Rowan Hamilton - Laracor -
Swift, Stella and Vanessa*

Only last week, walking the hushed fields
Of our most lovely Meath, now thinned by November,
I came to where the road from Laracor leads
To the Boyne river - that seemed more lake than river,
Stretched in uneasy light and stripped of reeds.
'Father and Son', F.R.Higgins

It is not difficult to find Trinity Well, the traditional source of
the Boyne. I went in search of it on a showery day in August
1985, the year so well remembered because of the exceptionally
cold and wet summer that had followed a harsh winter and
spring. I knew that the well was situated in the demesne of
Newbury Hall near Carbury, in County Kildare, and the
friendly owner, Richard Robinson, confirmed this for me when
I drove up his long front avenue and knocked at his hall door.
He showed me round this fine red-brick house, which was built
about 1750, and was probably designed by Nathaniel Clements,
a friend of the famous Richard Castle (or Cassels).

We talked about the bad weather, and Mr Robinson told me
how many of his neighbours had lost heavily on ruined crops.
He himself had little tillage, with the greater part of his three
hundred acres given over to cattle. In my ignorance, I said that
the weather wouldn't have affected him so badly, then. 'Of
course it did,' he answered. 'The cattle didn't thrive. How would
you like to be standing out all day in the rain? Cattle need the
sun, just like humans.'

I went back down the avenue and found Trinity Well where
he had directed me. It resembles the many other holy wells scat-

tered throughout Ireland, a stone surround, stone roof and basin, a sluggish trickle of water. Few of these wells earn a place in our centuries-old manuscript remains. However, there is a legend about this well and about the origin of the name 'Boyne' from Queen Boan, and this is recounted in the *Book of Lecan* and the *Book of Ballymote*, both compiled in the fifteenth century. The king of Leinster had a secret well in his garden. Anyone, save the king or his cup-bearers, approaching this well would be instantly deprived of sight. But Queen Boan, determined to test this magical power, approached the well and passed three times around it to the left. The spring rose and three enormous waves broke over Boan, mutilating her and blinding her. She fled towards the sea and was swept out on the waters of the river. Boan was the mother of Aengus, the Irish god of love, who dwelt in Brú na Bóinne, the Palace of the Boyne, at Newgrange.

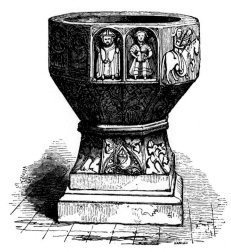

Clonard font, preserved in the local Church of Ireland church.
Clonard lies between Moyvalley and Kinnegad.

Ptolemy of Egypt, the second-century geographer, drew a map of Ireland and showed this river, calling it 'Bovinda'. Giraldus of Wales called it 'Boandus'. The quirky lexicographer of the Irish language, Father Dinneen, has this entry: 'Bóinn: an Irish goddess; the river Boyne'. Queen or goddess, this mythical personage belongs to the earliest prehistoric cycle of romance, pre-dating Cúchulainn and the epic of the cattle raid of Cooley.

No human habitation can be seen when one is standing beside this well. Westward rises the Hill of Carbury, crowned by a low tumulus, covering an unknown grave. Prehistoric Ireland broods all around.

I retraced my steps through the long wet grass to the drive and went on my way, following the stripling river to Boyne Bridge, then on through quiet Glynn Crossroads and into County Meath at the Boyne Aqueduct, where it is crossed by the Royal Canal and the railway, formerly the Midland Great Western line.

Three roads meet at Glynn, described by Sir William Wilde as 'a calm, peaceful, homestead spot, with Lady Well, a fountain dedicated to the Blessed Virgin, immediately adjoining the road, shaded by a splendid sycamore tree'. The peace and quiet remain, but Lady Well is neglected and gone dry. A splendid sycamore still towers over the well and set me wondering whether it was the same tree that Sir William admired 136 years before. Could a tree flourish for so long? Consulting my *Observer's Book of Trees*, I was delighted to read that there are no fixed limits to the life-span of trees and that oaks, for example, occasionally reach five hundred years.

Just past Glynn the road crosses the Boyne at Ballybogan Bridge, and from there to Trim, by following byroads, one can drive almost on a parallel course to the river. At Trim it broadens out as it sweeps past the massive ruins of the de Lacy castle.

Wilde was scathing about Trim. 'Of all the modern towns in Ireland of our acquaintance, we know few to vie with Trim in dirt, laziness and apathy ... It has the honour of being the county town, and possesses a gaol, a fever hospital, a poorhouse, barrack, court house and endowed school.' These public buildings recall the social conditions of the time, and as well, point very clearly to the colonial status of the country. The barrack, court house and gaol were there to ensure that the native inhabitants were kept in their place. The poor-house was the dreaded last refuge — if refuge is the right word — for the destitute.

Trim today, prosperous and busy, has won the Tidy Towns competition in 1972, 1974 and 1984. Access to the castle has been made easy and there are seats for the weary on a grassy

Trim Castle — a fine example of medieval
military architecture.

slope facing it. This immense fortress, extending over two acres, is one of the finest surviving examples of medieval military architecture in Ireland. In the Anglo-Norman invasion the Kingdom of Meath was granted to Hugh de Lacy, and about 1172 he made Trim his capital. A walled town grew up in the shadow and shelter of the castle. The great square keep, seventy-five feet high, with walls eleven feet thick, dominates the remains. A tower projects from the middle of each face of this keep. Considerable parts remain of the curtain wall enclosing the two-acre site, and include the gate-house and a number of flanking towers. The gate, with drawbridge, portcullis and barbican, is still in a fair state of preservation. The moat, now dry, was fed from the Boyne. Standing at the gate, one can easily visualise the crowds of men-at-arms, knights on horseback, servants and retainers of all kinds bustling in an out. It is best to walk to the side of the castle facing the river and so detach oneself in spirit from the present day, the better to capture the feeling of being back in medieval Ireland.

Being on the edge of the Pale, Trim was involved in the fortunes of invaders and defenders down the centuries. King John was there in 1210 trying to 'pacificate' de Lacy. In 1399 King Richard II imprisoned his cousins, Prince Hal (later King Henry V) and Humphrey of Gloucester, in the castle. Silken Thomas captured the castle and the town in 1537.

Not far away, across the river, the Yellow Steeple towers 125 feet high, a battered ruin, yet still retaining some of the

The Yellow Steeple, a fourteenth-century bell tower.

presence it had as a magnificent example of a fourteenth-century bell tower. It is the only part remaining of the great Augustinian monastery of St. Mary. Local tradition says that it was battered by Cromwell's cannon, but the same tradition names many ruins along the banks of the Boyne as having received the same attention.

The Duke of Wellington, then Arthur Wellesley, went to school at the Diocesan School in Abbey Lane. This fortified house, called Talbot Castle, was built by Sir John Talbot in 1415. It is now in use again as a private house. Wellesley was

Trim Castle — conjectural reconstruction of Trim Castle as it might have been around A.D. 1250. The round tower with projecting barbican spanning the moat is an unusual feature in the great curtain wall. A drawbridge was operated from the barbican.

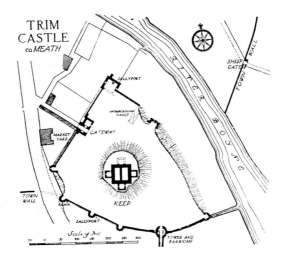

Member for Trim in the Irish Parliament from 1790 to 1795. A column has been erected in the town in his honour. Local piety keeps it in good repair. His contemporary, the writer Cesar Otway, is worth quoting about him. 'How different was the young fun-loving, comical, quizzing, gallanting Captain Arthur Wellesley, when residing in his shooting-lodge between Trim and Dangan, from the stern, cautious, care-worn Fabius of the Peninsular War; the trifling, provoking, capricious sprig of nobility, half-dreaded, half-doated on by the women, hated by the men, the dry joker, the practical wit, etc., from the redoubtable warrior of Waterloo — the great prime minister of England'.

The school was under the care of the Reverend James Hamilton, curate to the Vicar of Trim, and it was here that the greatest mathematical genius of the age received his early education. William Rowan Hamilton was a nephew of the Reverend James, and went to Trinity College, Dublin, from his uncle's school. He showed such prodigious intellectual powers that at the age of twenty-two, and while still an undergraduate, he was appointed Professor of Astronomy and superintendent of Dunsink Observatory. Soon after, he was made Astronomer Royal of Ireland. His greatest work, *The Elements of Quaternions*, was published posthumously in 1866.

The Vicar of Trim in those days was a hospitable and scholarly man called Richard Butler and the company at his vicarage often included Richard Lovell Edgeworth and his daughter Maria, the novelist, with the Beauforts of Navan. Of Maria the vicar wrote, 'We have now Maria Edgeworth with us as cheerful and fresh as ever and neither sadness nor ill-nature nor anything very bad can stand long in her presence'. Her father, Richard Lovell, was a noted eccentric who meddled inexcusably in his daughter's work, but not even this interference could overshadow the genius of the admirable Maria, nor change her nature. Her simple and unaffected goodness captivated all she met, from Sir Walter Scott to the poorest tenant on her father's estate.

When we visit Navan, we shall speak further of the great sailor and hydrographer, Sir Francis Beaufort, who was born there in 1774.

From military exploits and imposing castles it is but a short distance downriver to the vast ruins of the medieval cathedral of Meath at Newtown Trim. This dates from 1206 and must have been one of the largest churches of its time in Ireland. Pasture land slopes down for about a hundred yards to the placid river, and doubtless the Augustinian canons who were in charge here took many a fine salmon from it. As you come in from the stile beside the main road, you first meet a thirteenth-century parish church. Step inside the walls and you will see a fine late sixteenth-century altar tomb, with effigies of Sir Luke Dillon and his wife, recumbent side by side.

Now you must cross the river by the old five-arched St Peter's bridge, which is so narrow that only one vehicle at a time can cross it and there are traffic lights at each end. Turn back towards Trim and stop at the Echo sign opposite the cathedral ruins. Your 'halloo' across the river comes echoing back to you with startling clearness from the walls of the ancient refectory.

Taking the road to Navan, you pass by the old bridge again and see just below it the ruins of another church, the Friary of St. John the Baptist, an Augustinian foundation of the thirteenth century. Here again inviting meadows slope gently down to the river. It is good to see workmen from the Office of Public Works engaged in the restoration and maintenance of these ancient monuments.

Dillon Monument, a late sixteenth-century altar tomb.

It is well worthwhile to pause at St. Peter's Bridge and look back towards Trim, barely a mile distant; all the great ruins described above can be seen from this point. Then one should walk or drive slowly back to the town, where the Yellow Steeple and the mighty castle stand out on the skyline in all their majesty.

A couple of miles' journey on a side road south from Trim

brings one to Laracor, with which the name of Jonathan Swift is forever associated. In 1700 Swift, then thirty-two, was presented with the vicarage of Laracor and two other livings. The easy-going practices of the Church of Ireland then did not require him to spend all or indeed much of his time at Laracor. He took up residence there in September 1701, but spent the years from 1707 to 1709 in London. He was back in Laracor in July 1709 but stayed only until September of the following year. From 1710 to 1713 he lived in London, gaining fame and influence as a political pamphleteer. He was appointed Dean of St. Patrick's Cathedral in Dublin in April 1713 and spent from July to September of that year at Laracor. This is his last recorded stay there.

Nothing remains of the church in which he ministered, nor of the cottage nearby in which Stella (Esther Johnson) and Rebecca Dingley lived. The present church is no longer in use for religious purposes and is now a private house. The interior has been converted into a dwelling of unusual and attractive design. Stella and her companion were living at Laracor during the years 1710 to 1713 when Swift wrote to them the delightful letters which were published after his death under the title *Journal to Stella*. He was then at the peak of his career in London, a welcome visitor in many great houses and a confidant of ministers of the Crown.

Judging by these long and gossipy letters, this was probably the happiest time of his life. They were addressed, out of prudence, to both ladies and recount the events of his days in London — where he dined and who was of the company, what the weather was like, enquiries after their health and affectionate scoldings for dilatoriness on their part in writing to him. He writes with eighteenth-century candour: 'Mrs. Tisdall is very big, ready to lie down. Her husband is a puppy. Do his feet stink still?' and sometimes with a humour that might be called broad: ''tis still terribly cold. I wish my very cold hand was in the warmest place about you, young women. I'd give ten guineas on that account with all my heart, faith.' In places he uses a special 'little language', addressing them as 'MD', which is taken to mean 'my dears'. The description of himself as 'Presto' was inserted by an early editor in place of the puzzling 'Pdfr' which may have meant 'poor dear foolish rogue'. 'Presto' was the punning name given to Swift by the Duchess of Shrewsbury, who was an Italian and could not pronounce his real name. His delight in Laracor is shown in a letter of February 1711. 'I should be plaguy busy at Laracor if I were there now, cutting down willows, planting others, scouring my canal, and every kind of thing. If Raymond [Dr. Raymond, Vicar of Trim] goes over this summer, you must submit, and make them a visit, that we may have another eel and trout fishing; and that Stella may ride by and see Presto in his morning-gown in the garden.' And again: 'O that we were at Laracor this fine day. The willows begin to peep, and the quicks to bud. My dreams out; I was a-dreaming last night that I eat ripe cherries. And now they begin to catch the pikes, and will shortly the trouts (Pox on these ministers), and I would fain know whether the floods were ever so high as to get over the holly bank or the river walk; if so, then all my pikes are gone; but I hope not.'

Passing along the quiet road from the site of Stella's cottage to the crossroads where the church stands, it is easy to imagine the young vicar of Laracor taking the air with his two friends, Mrs. Dingley and Mrs. Johnson, as Stella was called (it was a courtesy of the time to give unmarried ladies the title 'Mrs' when they reached a certain — or uncertain — age). His friendship with Vanessa (Esther van Homrigh) was ten years in the future; it ripened in the heady years in London between 1710 and 1713 when he saw a great deal of Mrs. van Homrigh and her daughter, a beautiful and vivacious young woman half his age. But even in London he wrote to Stella:'Do you know one thing that I find I can write politics to you much easier than to anybody else? But I swear my head is full and I wish I were at Laracor with dear charming MD.'

Did his friendship with Vanessa come to a climax when she followed him to Dublin in 1714 after he became Dean of St. Patrick's? 'Discretion! Discretion!' he enjoined on her, writing in great unease. 'I ever feared the tattle of this nasty town.'

Jonathan Swift, Dean of St. Patrick's Cathedral, Dublin. Author of *Gulliver's Travels* and many other works. Satirist and powerful pamphleteer against mis-government of Ireland by England.

Below: Hester Johnson, called 'Stella' by Jonathan Swift, lived for a while at Laracor in County Meath. The delightful *Journal to Stella*, letters written to her by Swift when he was in London, reveal his longing to be with her in the peace and tranquility of rural Meath.

Below left: Esther van Homrigh fell madly in love with Swift on meeting him in London and followed him to Dublin when he became Dean of St. Patrick's Cathedral. Swift called her 'Vanessa'; his poem 'Cadenus and Vanessa' is an account of their friendship.

His friendship with Stella was of much longer standing. He had first met her in 1689 when he became secretary to Sir William Temple, a retired English diplomat living at Moor Park in Surrey. She was the daughter of a former steward whose widow was companion to Sir William's sister. Stella was only eight years old then and Swift was twenty-one. He taught her to write and directed her reading. After he had returned to Ireland to take up residence at Laracor, he advised Stella, then twenty, to remove to Ireland where her small legacy from Sir William would go much further.

He was greatly affected by her death at forty-seven in 1728, 'the death of the truest, most virtuous and most valuable friend that I, or perhaps any other person, ever was blessed with'. His verses on her thirty-sixth birthday are those of a friend, rather than a lover:

> Then, Chloe, still go on to prate
> Of thirty-six and thirty-eight;
> Pursue your trade of scandal-picking,
> Your hints, that Stella is no chicken;
> Your innuendos, when you tell us
> That Stella loves to talk with fellows;
> And let me warn you to believe
> A truth, for which your soul should grieve;
> That should you live to see the day
> When Stella's locks must all be grey,
> When age must print a furrowed trace
> On every feature of her face;
> That you, and all your senseless tribe,
> Could art, or time, or nature bribe
> To make you look like beauty's queen,
> And hold forever at fifteen;
> No bloom of youth can ever blind
> The cracks and wrinkles of your mind;
> All men of sense will pass your door,
> And crowd to Stella's at four-score.

The relations between Stella, Vanessa and Swift remain one of the greatest mysteries in literary history. Was he married to Stella, and if so, why did he keep it a secret? Was Vanessa his mistress and did she bear a child by him? Did he have a tremendous row with Vanessa late in 1724? If he did, what caused it and did it precipitate her death a few months later? All that can be said with certainty is that there was an abiding friendship between himself and Stella, highly valued by both of them, and that Vanessa was madly in love with him.

Some of Swift's letters to Vanessa have survived, but neither they nor his poem 'Cadenus and Vanessa' throw any light on the mystery surrounding their relationship. Again and again he urges her to be discreet and even writes: 'If you are in Ireland while I am there, I shall see you very seldom.' Her letters to him are clearly those of a woman very much in love and tormented by the constraints of the discretion he has imposed on her.

'Not to marry a young Woman.' This is one of the grim resolutions for old age written by Swift many years before he met Vanessa. And those two beautiful young women who loved him so dearly were dead for many years when he wrote his 'Verses on the Death of Dr. Swift':

> My female Friends, whose tender Hearts,
> Have better learn'd to Act their Parts,
> Receive the News in doleful Dumps,
> 'The Dean is Dead, (and what is Trumps?).

This is the Dean best known for the rage and savage indignation that lacerated his heart. It is not the Presto in the 'little language' of the *Journal to Stella*.

Like all parishes of former days, Laracor buried its dead in the grounds of the church. Young children were playing around the tombstones as I took my last look at the place so dear to Jonathan Swift.

Chapter 2

Bective Abbey - Mary Lavin - Hill of Tara - O'Connell's Monster Meeting - 1798 Rising - Fionn Mac Cumhaill - Legend of Diarmuid and Gráinne

Beautiful was the appearance of Cormac in that assembly ... symmetrical and beautiful of form, without blemish or reproach.
'Cormac Mac Airt Presiding at Tara', Douglas Hyde

From Laracor I took the road to Bective, five miles to the northeast. The few houses near the crossroads hardly earn the name of village, but no doubt there were more people living there in former times, when the Cistercians were in residence in the great abbey. Turning left at the crossroads, I crossed the Boyne at Bective Bridge and saw the ruins of the abbey on high ground overlooking bridge and river, a fine site evidently chosen with care.

The name Bective Bridge instantly recalled Mary Lavin's first collected volume of short stories, *Tales from Bective Bridge*, and I remembered that she had lived in her early married years on the abbey farm beside these ruins. In his introduction to the *Tales*, Lord Dunsany, who had encouraged both Francis Ledwidge and Mary Lavin, wrote, 'These two great writers, as I believe them to be, both wrote to me, by a strange coincidence, from the same bank of the same river, the left bank of the Boyne,' and he remarked on her 'vivid appreciation of the beauty of the fields'. Even more striking, to one reader at least, is the way Mary Lavin brings her characters to life and illuminates their condition in a few words. In 'The Dead Soldier' a mother, left alone with her daughter after her sons have died or left home, says: 'Listen to the wind under the door. I wish there was a man in the house to put a bit of cement on the floor there, by the hinge.' And the Irish absorption with death has rarely been better evoked than in these two sentences: 'Your father was the handsomest corpse that ever was stretched. People that never knew him when he was alive came from miles just to see him laid out, he was such a handsome sight.'

In these stories there are no set descriptions of scenery or views, or rhapsodies about the beautiful river, but one is conscious all the time of the dominating role of the land in the lives of the people. It is impossible today to move through the by-roads of Meath without feeling that power of the land.

The Cistercian abbey at Bective was richly endowed, owning 240 acres, a mill and a fishing weir on the Boyne. Founded in 1150 by Murchad O Maeilsheachlainn, King of Meath, it was a daughter house of Mellifont, the first Cistercian monastery in Ireland, and was dedicated to the Blessed Virgin. The abbot sat in the Parliament of the Pale, being a temporal as well as a spiritual lord.

When the dissolution of the monasteries and the transfer of all their property to the Crown began in 1535, Bective was one of the first to be suppressed, no doubt because of its nearness to Dublin, and it passed from ecclesiastical ownership in 1536. The lands were first leased to a Thomas Asgarde and subsequently passed to the Dillons and then to the Boltons.

The ruins are an impressive sight, with turrets, gables and a square battlemented tower. A padlocked iron gate at the roadside has an inset wicket gate closed only by a latch, and then one crosses a field and a stile to reach the abbey. In the fifteenth century the building was fortified and the present cloisters and many of the surrounding apartments were added. It is worth the visit just to see the beautiful Early English cinquefoil arches in the cloisters. A feature pleasing to visitors is the plan of the abbey fixed to the top of a low, square pillar in the cloisters. This plan, prepared by the Office of Public Works, names the different parts of the building and shows their date of construction.

On a quiet summer's day, the only sounds to be heard are the occasional burst of birdsong and the low murmur from the weir

Early English cinquefoil arches in the cloister of Bective Abbey.

on the Boyne.

From Bective Abbey I went in search of Clady Bridge, said to be the oldest in Ireland, and after many enquiries locally, eventually found it. You must go about half-way down the front avenue of Bective House, and, keeping a sharp lookout, you will see a rough path off it on the right-hand side. The path peters out after a few yards and then you must plough your way through deep grass and nettles. The bridge is heavily overgrown but the two arches can be seen and it is possible to walk across. It is only five feet wide and has no parapet, hence its description as a footbridge, and it does look as if it has been there from the beginning of time. It may have been built to give access across the Clady river to an old church of which only vestiges now remain.

Clady Bridge, reputed to be the oldest bridge in Ireland.

I retraced my path to Bective Abbey, then across the bridge to the crossroads, where a signpost pointing to Tara set me on the next stage on my journey back into time and history.

A long, straight, narrow road takes one to the entrance gate to the Hill of Tara, and from here it is an easy climb up a sloping field to the ringfort known as Cormac's House, on which stands the Lia Fáil and a deplorable, badly-weathered modern statue of St. Patrick. From this vantage point there is a fine view of the countryside, and the strategic, commanding position of the hill is very evident. The other remaining earthworks, ringforts and ramparts can be seen to the north but nothing remains of the buildings that housed royal assemblages and feasts in the prehistoric Ireland of thousands of years ago. They were probably made of wood or wattle and daub, and as Tara was abandoned by the high king Maelsheachlainn in A.D. 1022, all traces of these structures have long since disappeared.

So there is very little to see on the Hill of Tara. The Lia Fáil, a granite pillar stone about five feet over ground, was the inauguration stone for the kings and according to tradition it roared when the king was accepted. In the graveyard near the road you may see another stone, called St. Adamnáin's Cross, with a figure of the kind known as a *Síle na Gig* (a pre-Christian fertility symbol) carved in relief. Some authorities interpret this stone as a representation of the Celtic god, Cernunnos. The Protestant church in this graveyard contains a medieval window and another window by Evie Hone. And that is all. Now you must call on your imagination to re-create here the Tara of great assemblies, of kings and warriors, of music and song. Does anyone now remember or sing Thomas Moore's 'The Harp That Once Through Tara's Halls'?

> The harp that once through Tara's halls,
> The soul of music shed,
> Now hangs as mute on Tara's walls,
> As if that soul were fled ...
> No more to chiefs and ladies bright
> The harp of Tara swells.

Tom, the darling of London drawing-rooms, was no historian, but he did have a sense of his country's heroic past, even if he expressed that sense in songs that now seem little more than sentimental vapourings.

In the rigidly stratified society in Ireland in the period from the first to the ninth centuries, seating arrangements in banqueting halls were prescribed by precise protocol. The long, hollow area you see at the northern end of the hill has been called the 'banqueting hall', though on no great authority. It is seventy feet wide and about seven hundred feet long and could

Aerial view of Tara. The Hill of Tara, setting for royal assemblages and feasts in prehistoric Ireland thousands of years ago. Here Daniel O'Connell held the largest of his monster meetings, attended by nearly a million people.

conceivably have been the site of a long house of the type described in medieval literature.

The door of the 'banqueting hall' faced east, and beside it was stationed the king's bodyguard of mercenary soldiers. Envoys were placed west of the king. After them came guest companies, then poets, then harpers. A harper ranked as a freeman, because of his art, but other musicians, pipers, horn players and jugglers were not free. They sat at the corner near the door, beside the mercenaries. In the other half of the hall, a warrior and a champion guarded the door, to prevent any disturbance. The king's noble clients sat west of these, in attendance on the king. Then the hostages were seated after them; a *brehon* (judge) after them and then the king's wife. Hostages whose lives were forfeit were placed in chains in the corner furthest from the door where the king could watch them.

A great feast was held by each king at the beginning of his reign, to symbolise his marriage to Medb, or Maeve, who was really a goddess and not a human, and this custom continued down to the sixth century. Legend merges into recorded history in the story of Tara; its period of greatest glory extended from the reign of Cormac Mac Airt in the third century to the middle of the sixth century.

The statue of St. Patrick was placed, one supposes, to commemorate the encounter on Tara between the saint and King Laoghaire on Easter Sunday. On his way to face the king and his druids, Patrick and his companions chanted a hymn called the 'Deer's Cry' as they assumed the shape of deer to avoid assassination. This hymn, also called 'The Breastplate of Patrick' has survived in an eighth-century manuscript and the passage that begins 'Christ with me, Christ before me, Christ behind me, Christ in me' is well known, but the story is, of course, apocryphal.

Tara declined in importance after the sixth century, and this decline is attributed to the cursing of the place by St. Ruadhán of Lorrha. The legend relates that King Diarmuid decreed that the door of every chieftain's house should be a spear's length wide. A chieftain called Guaire was found to have a doorway too

Seating plan for a banquet at Tara — from an old manuscript.

Horsemen, or charioteers, and stewards :—cuinn for them.	Distributors (or dividers) :— a *mael* for them.	Cupbearers:— a *mael* for them Herdsmen :— a *mael* for them.		Charioteers :—crooked bones for them. Steward :—cuind for him.
Harpers and timpanists :—a pig's shoulder for them.	Pipers :— a *colptha* for them.	Fire. Chess-players :— a *colptha* for them.		Hunters :—a pig's shoulder for them.
Brehons :—a *lon-chroichti* for them.	Scolaige :—a *less-croichte* for them.	Fire. Drink-bearers :—a *les-chroichti* for them.		Aire forgill :—a *lon-chroichte* for them.
Professor of Literature :—a *lon-chroichti*. Tanist professor:—a *les-crochait* or *prim-chrochait*.	Artisans :—an *ir-croichte* for them.	Braziers :—an *ir-croichti* for them. Fools :—an *ir-croichti* for them.		Ruiri :—a *lon-croichte* for them. Queen and royal *ruireach* :—a *les-croichte* [for them].
Ollam poet :—a *loarce* for him. Anrudh [poet] :—a crooked bone.	Smiths :—a *mael* for them.	Fire. Vat. Physicians and mariners :— a *mael* for them.		Aire ard :—a *loarc* for them. Cli [poets] :—a crooked bone for them.
Briugu and aire tuisi :—a *laracc* for them.	Shield-makers :—a *milgitain* for them.	Mariners :—a *milgitain* for them.		Aire tuisi :—a crooked bone. Historian :—a *loarc* for him.
Augtarsair :—a pig's shoulder. His tanist :—a crooked bone.	Chariot-makers :—a *milgitain* for them.	Candle. Creacoire :—crooked bones for them, or pig's *colptha*.		Aire desa :—a *colptha* for them. Dos [poet] :—a pig's shoulder. Or thus: Carpenters and *airig echta*.
Augurs, druids, and comail :— a *colptha* for them.	Jugglers :—a pig's *colptha* for them.	Buffoons :—a pig's *colptha* for them.		Fochloc [poet] :—an *ir-croichte* for him. Or : aire desa.
House-builder, carpenter, and *sair-churan*, and rath-builder :—an *ir-crochti* for them.	Satirists :—the fat [part of the] shoulder for them.	Lamp. Braigitoire :—the fat [part of the] shoulder for them.		Cooks, and creccoire or cornaire :—midh mir.
Trumpeters, and footmen, or house-builders :—cheering mead for them.				Rath-builder and oblaire :— a *milgitain* for them.
Engravers and ring-makers :— a *milgatan* for them.		Common Hall.		Aire echta :—a pig's shoulder. Canu [poet] :—a crooked bone.
Shoe-makers and turners :—the fat [part of the] shoulder for them.	The King's doorkeepers :—and chines for them.	The King's fools :—backs for them.		Muirighi, and clasaighi :—the fat [part of the] shoulder.

Door.

narrow, but when the king's envoy sought to widen it, Guaire killed him and then fled to his uncle, Ruadhán, for protection. But the king violated this sanctuary and, seizing Guaire, brought him in chains to Tara. The incensed Ruadhán appeared at Tara and cursed it, thus destroying it. It is probable that the spread of Christianity hastened the decline of pagan festivals at Tara.

Daniel O'Connell selected the Hill of Tara for the largest of all of his famous 'monster meetings', that held on 15 August 1843, in the campaign for the repeal of the union. Gavan Duffy wrote: 'The number is supposed to have reached between 500,000 and 750,000 persons. It was ordinarily spoken of as a million, and was certainly a muster of men such as had never before assembled in one place in Ireland, in peace or war.' O'Connell, in his expansive way, put the number at a million and a half.

It must have been a wonderful sight on that glorious day. They came from far and near, in carriages, in jaunting cars, in farm wagons, on foot and on horseback. Ten thousand horsemen were in attendance on the Liberator. The route from Dublin led through towns and villages, and at each the local muster, led by their band, joined the march. Those who had come from distant parts had camped overnight in the green pastures of Meath, and now joined in. The repealers of Kells, Trim and Navan swelled the throng, carrying brightly-coloured banners. The vehicles had to be abandoned three miles from the hill, as there was no room for them there. The crowd was mustered by mounted marshals, wearing distinctive badges, and the discipline and good order of the multitude was remarkable. Gavan Duffy continues: 'The procession, however, was but as a river discharging itself into an ocean. The whole district was covered with men. The population within a day's march began to arrive on foot shortly after daybreak and continued by every available approach, until noon. Hill and plain were covered with a multitude "countless as the bearded grain".' Remember that this meeting was held when the population was close to eight million, and before the Great Famine had swept over the land.

The event was celebrated in a rousing ballad:

> On the fifteenth day of August in the year of '43,
> This glorious day, I well may say, recorded it shall be,
> On the Royal Hill of Tara, Irish thousands did prevail,
> In Union's bands to join their hands with Dan for the
>   Repeal.

In one verse the balladeer refers to the 'Croppies' Grave'. In the Rising of 1798, eight thousand United Irishmen in green cockades had established themselves on the Hill of Tara. It was the last week of May in that summer of glorious weather and appalling atrocities. Forty campfires blazed on the hill that night and the men feasted on great quantities of boiled mutton and other plunder from the fertile plains below them. They had seized a quantity of arms and ammunition from a Scotch Fencibles regiment and captured the ten Highlanders who were guarding it. Here on this royal seat of kings, ready to free their country and restore its ancient glory, their spirits soared and they sent a defiant message to the commander of the local yeomanry. They held a strong, well-chosen position, but in the event this did not compensate for their lack of experience and military skill. Late in the evening they were attacked by a force of Fencibles and local yeomen, numbering three hundred in all, who toiled up the hill dragging their one piece of artillery, a six-pounder. These government forces met with a spirited resistance and in a final effort to avoid defeat, their commander, Captain Blanche, ordered a desperate last charge. In trying to seize the six-pounder, the rebels exposed themselves beyond the walls and earthworks. Blanche opened fire with the cannon and the rebels fell in great numbers. The survivors fled the field, leaving 350 dead and great quantities of pikes, muskets, swords and reaping hooks. Blanche's losses amounted to only thirteen men killed and twenty-eight wounded. Many years after this disaster, the Lia Fáil was taken from its original position near the Mound of the Hostages and re-erected in its present position in honour of the men who died on the hill in 1798.

Today no more peaceful scene presents itself than this great hill with its mysterious mounds, monuments of a history going back thousands of years. A dozen sheep scampered away from me as I walked down to the gate, and the vengeful lines of the anonymous eighteenth-century poet came into my mind.

Tá an Teamhair ina fhéir agus féach an Traoi mar atá,
Is na Sasanaigh féin, is féidir go bhfuighidís bás.

(See Troy and Tara, where in grass they lie,
Even the very English might yet die.)
(Trans. Máire Mhac an tSaoi)

From the gate, a glimpse of the river two miles to the north-west reminded me that the Boyne had a central place in the pleasing legend concerning Fionn Mac Cumhaill, which relates how he acquired his great wisdom and knowledge. The story is told in the collection known as *The Boyhood Exploits of Fionn*, part of the great mythological cycle of the Fianna, the band of professional soldiers who lived exclusively for war and hunting. Fionn's father, who was leader of the Fianna, had been killed in battle by Goll Mac Morna, and Fionn's mother put him in the care of two wise women. His education would not have been complete without a knowledge of poetry, and so the women brought him to study under Finn-eigeas, a poet of renown who lived on the banks of the Boyne. Near where he lived there was a dark pool in the river, called the pool Feic, and the Salmon of Knowledge lived in this pool. Above the pool a large hazel tree stretched its branches over the river and from the branches nuts of knowledge fell into the water and were eaten by the Salmon. It was foretold that whoever ate the Salmon would acquire great wisdom and gifts of magic and prophecy.

It happened that Finn-eigeas succeeded in catching the Salmon while Fionn was living with him and he asked Fionn to cook it for him but warned him on no account to eat even the smallest morsel. Fionn built a fire of sticks on the banks of the river and watched the Salmon carefully as it cooked. He saw a small blister rise on it and tried to press it down with his thumb and scalded himself. He thrust his thumb into his mouth, sucking and chewing it to ease the burning sensation. Then he brought the fish to Finn-eigeas to eat, but when the poet learned what had happened he told Fionn that he could teach him no more since he had eaten of the fish and that he would become a great leader of the Fianna. Ever after, when Fionn was in difficulties and needed guidance, all he had to do was put his thumb in his mouth and suck it, and instantly his proper course became clear to him.

Fionn was known as 'The Golden Salmon', and 'lived two hundred years in flourishing condition and thirty more years free of debility before he took the leap of his old age'. The legend goes that in order to test his strength, he tried to leap across the Boyne but fell and was dashed between two rocks. Fishermen dragged out his body with gaffs and cut off his head.

Fionn was equally renowned as poet and as warrior, and most of the early poems in the manuscripts were ascribed to him. One of the collections is known as *The Poem Book of Fionn*, and was written, according to notes on the margin, by three different scribes at Louvain during the years 1620-27 for a Captain Sorley MacDonnell, an Irish soldier who was probably on foreign service at the time.

'May Day' is one of Fionn's best known poems; its quality may be judged from the following prose translation of some verses from it:

> May day, fair aspect, perfect season.
> Blackbirds sing a full lay when the sun casts a meagre
>   beam.
> The strenuous corncrake speaks; the high pure cataract
>   sings of joy from the warm water;
> rustling of rushes has come.
>
> Man flourishes, the maiden buds in her fair strong pride.
> Perfect each forest from top to ground; perfect each great
>   stately plain.
> Fierce ardour and riding of horses; the serried host is
>   ranged around.
> *(Trans. Gerard Murphy)*

One of the most famous stories in the Fenian cycle, *The Pursuit of Diarmuid and Gráinne*, begins in the banqueting hall of Tara. It is a story of love and betrayal, of high chivalry, the loyalty of comrades and the fickleness and wiles of one woman.

Fionn Mac Cumhaill comes to Tara in his old age, after the death of his wife, seeking the hand in marriage of Gráinne, the young daughter of King Cormac Mac Airt. Cormac gives a splendid feast to welcome Fionn, and Gráinne sees him for the first time in the banqueting hall. She is astonished that this old man should desire her, and instantly makes up her mind to escape the fate being arranged for her. She sends her slave-girl attendant to the *grianán* (women's house or literally 'sunny place') for a goblet which she fills with wine. The slave-girl brings it to Fionn and the king and most of the guests. When they drink from it they fall into a deep sleep. Gráinne goes to Fionn's son, Oisín, and offers herself to him but he refuses her. She then offers herself to Diarmuid O Duibhne but he, too, refuses her. She puts Diarmuid under *'geasa'*, strong druidical bonds, to take her away with him that night. A hero who failed to observe *geasa* would be shamed forever.

Diarmuid bore a love-spot on his forehead and no warrior of the Fianna was more desired by the women of Ireland. In an eleventh-century manuscript the following is attributed to Gráinne:

> There's a man I would wish to see,
> For whom I would give the golden earth,
> All, all, though it were an empty bargain.
> *(Trans. David Greene)*

Gráinne slips out through a door in the *grianán*, leaving Diarmuid under *geasa* to follow her. Diarmuid seeks counsel from his Fianna comrades. Oisín tells him that he is not responsible for the druidic bonds and that he should go with Gráinne, but warns him against the vengeful treachery of Fionn. Oscar also advises him to follow Gráinne, for only a worthless wretch would break his bond. Caoilte says that although he himself has a fitting wife, he would forsake all if Gráinne offered him her love. Finally, Diorraing tells him to follow Gráinne until his death comes of it.

Diarmuid leaps over the wall of the banqueting hall to join the waiting Gráinne. The story continues with their wandering through Ireland, pursued by Fionn who is consumed with hate and jealousy of Diarmuid.

As they hide from him, Gráinne lulls Diarmuid to sleep with the poem 'Lullaby of Adventurous Love', which begins:

> Sleep a little, a little little,
> for you have little to fear,
> lad I gave love to ...
> *(Trans. and title, David Greene)*

William Butler Yeats was inspired by this poem to write his 'Lullaby':

> Beloved, may your sleep be sound
> That have found it where you fed.
> What were all the world's alarms
> To mighty Paris when he found
> Sleep upon a golden bed,
> That first dawn in Helen's arms?

Aengus, the god of love, carries Gráinne off to his mansion, Brú na Bóinne (Newgrange), when she is in danger of being seized by Fionn.

The pursuit ends on Ben Gulban, County Sligo, where Diarmuid, incited by Fionn, hunts a wild boar in defiance of *geasa* laid on him by Aengus, his foster father, and is mortally wounded in the chase. As Diarmuid lies dying, he reminds Fionn that since the day he had eaten of the Salmon of Knowledge from the Boyne, he could cure any wound or illness by a drink from his cupped hands. There is a well nearby and Fionn goes reluctantly to fetch a drink for Diarmuid. As he is returning, a thought of Gráinne comes to him and he opens his hands and lets the water spill on the ground. Oscar threatens to kill him unless he brings a drink to Diarmuid, but as he comes to him again with the water, Diarmuid dies. The Fianna give three great shouts of lamentation over the body of the dead hero. Then Aengus comes and bears it away to his palace on the Boyne.

Not long after, Fionn sought out Gráinne and 'left not plying her with sweet words and loving, gentle discourses until he brought her to his will'. When the Fianna saw Fionn returning to them with Gráinne on his arm, they let one great shout of scorn and derision and Gráinne hung her head in shame. Oisín said sarcastically, 'On my word, Fionn, you will watch Gráinne well from this day forth.'

Gráinne is shown in this story as fickle and vain, in contrast to Diarmuid who is chivalrous, high-minded and brave. Gráinne's father, Cormac Mac Airt, had a low opinion of women in general. In his 'Instructions' which come to us in a ninth-century manuscript, he devotes sixty lines to a catalogue of women's faults. These five lines, from a translation by Kuno Meyer, are typical of the list:

> They are crabbed as constant companions,
> Viragoes in strife,
> Exceeding all bounds in keeping others waiting,
> Not to be trusted with a secret,
> Better to trample on them than to fondle them.

Nevertheless, when his son Cairbre asked him 'What is the sweetest thing you have heard?', Cormac's answer was:

> The shout of triumph after victory,
> Praise after wages,
> A lady's invitation to her pillow.

I rouse myself from this dream of heroic Ireland and face down the hill to where the Boyne winds towards the Brú of Aengus.

CHAPTER 3

Tailteann - Kells - Tara Mines - Sir Peter Warren -
Sir William Johnson - Sir Francis Beaufort - Athlumney
Castle - Navan - the Ramparts Walk

> Then, on a page made golden as the crown
> Of sainted man, a scripture you enscroll
> Blackly, firmly, with the quickened skill
> Lessoned by famous masters in our school,
> And with an ink whose lustre will keep fresh
> For fifty generations of our flesh.
> *'The Book of Kells', Padraig Colum*

Here in Navan we are only ten miles from Kells, whence came that wonder of illuminated manuscripts, the Book of Kells, and where we can see some fine high crosses. Half-way to Kells, we stop to pay our respects to the Hill of Tailte, where the famed Tailteann Fair and Games were held. *The Annals of the Four Masters* record that 'in the reign of Lugh Lámhfhada [Lugh of the Long Hand], the fair of Tailteann was established in commemoration and in remembrance of his foster-mother Tailte, daughter of the King of Spain and wife of Eochaidh, son of Erc, the last king of the Firbolgs.' It continued down to the time of Roderick O'Connor, the last High King of Ireland, who hosted the games and celebrations there in a ceremonial way for the last time in A.D.1168. According to Sir William Wilde, the fair continued on a smaller and more informal scale until the middle of the eighteenth century.

Gatherings like that at Tailte were a feature of life in Ireland from pre-Christian times. Edmund Spenser in his *View of the State of Ireland* written in 1594 but not published until 1633, observes, 'There is a great use amongst the Irish to make great assemblies together upon a rath or built house to parlie (as they say) about matters and wrongs between township and township or one private person and another.'

According to tradition, much more varied activities were carried on at Tailte than the limited kind described by Spenser. There was music and dancing, athletic contests and recitations of poetry, genealogy and tales of goddesses and heroes. The story of the origin of Aonach Tailteann and the accounts of the proceedings there are very much in the realm of legend, rather than history, but as one sees the large earthen fort on the top of the grassy hill, sloping upwards from the Blackwater, one recalls some of the pleasing legends which have come down to us.

One of the most interesting is that concerning the marriages or betrothals that took place at the Aonach each August. The young men and women were first arranged in separate and opposite lines. Following this opportunity of taking a good look at one another, they moved down to a hollow and took station there on either side of a high wall. There was a door in this wall with a small hole in it, through which each young woman passed her middle finger. The men on the other side looked at it, and if one admired it, he took hold of it and the owner then became his bride. Sir William Wilde writes, 'So we find a fair and pretty hand, a delicate and taper finger, with its snowy skin and delicately formed nail, were even more captivating among the Irish lads and lasses some twelve hundred years ago than they are at the present day.' But, alas for romantic love, the marriage held good for only a year and a day. If the couple disagreed during that time they returned to Tailte, stood back to back in the fort, one facing north, the other south, and walked out a divorced couple, free to try their luck again in the marriage hollow. Social historians may note Sir William's final comment: 'What a pity there is no Teltown marriage in the present day! What numbers would take advantage of it!' This legend echoes the Brehon laws on marriage and divorce in a somewhat debased and simplified version, for those old Irish laws laid down strict and detailed provisions as to property and other rights which found no place, apparently, in the 'Teltown marriage'.

An attempt was made in the early years of the Free State to

revive the festival, and Tailteann Games were held in 1928 and 1932. These were mainly devoted to sport, although Oliver St. John Gogarty won a gold medal in 1928 for his volume of poems, *An Offering of Swans*.

We press onwards to Kells, now officially known by its Irish name, Ceanannas Mór, meaning the 'great fort'. This is an old town, so old, indeed, that it is mentioned as a royal residence for the high kings centuries before the coming of St. Patrick. The renowned Cormac Mac Airt came to live at Kells for a while when he resigned his kingship after losing an eye in a battle at Tara, a blemish which barred him from holding high office in prehistoric Ireland.

Colmcille founded a monastery here about A.D.559 and in 806 the monks of Iona, off the coast of Scotland, came to Kells when they were forced by Viking raids to flee their own monastery. Some scholars believe that the Book of Kells was written and illuminated in Iona and brought to Kells, possibly in an unfinished state, when the monks sought refuge there. After many

Kells Cross, a scriptural cross in Market Street.

vicissitudes, and following the dissolution of the monasteries by Henry VIII in 1539, it was safely lodged in Trinity College Library in 1661, and it remains one of the great treasures of that library. Another heirloom, the Kells crozier, one of the finest examples of Irish metalwork of the tenth century, is now in the British Museum.

Kells itself suffered from many Viking raids in the ninth, tenth and eleventh centuries. Then the Normans came and looted and burned the monastery, and in 1315 Edward Bruce

Kells Monastery — conjectural reconstruction of the monastery at Kells as it might have been around A.D.1100. The circular enclosure bounded by a stone or earthen bank was a feature of these settlements.

in his march south burned the town to the ground. With that turbulent history in mind, it is a relief to find here, in astonishingly good condition, a round tower, high crosses and the building known as St. Columb's House. The first cross we meet is the Market Cross, which stands at a crossing three-quarters of the way up the hilly street leading to the Protestant church and the round tower. As I examined it a woman, laden with shopping bags, paused to get her breath, and her three small children perched on the base of the cross looking curiously at the carved figures. Those at the base, which the children could see most clearly, show horsemen, a battle scene and a number of animals. This is a scriptural cross, with scenes from the Old and New Testaments — Adam and Eve, Cain and Abel, Daniel in the Lion's Den, the sacrifice of Isaac and Christ in the tomb, guarded by soldiers. The crucifixion shows Christ without a halo, which with other characteristics indicates that the cross dates from the eighth or ninth century.

We walk up Market Street to the churchyard with the round tower dominating its far end. The tower is almost one hundred feet high, with a doorway ten feet from the ground. At the top there are five windows instead of the usual four; the explanation given is that five were required to command a view of the five roads leading to Kells.

Nearby is the South Cross, adorned with a wealth of ornamentation showing scriptural scenes in striking detail, as for example the men with long forks piling logs on the fire in the carving of the Children in the Fiery Furnace. In front of the church stands the shaft of the West Cross, the top and arms of which are missing. The carvings on this cross are particularly fine. Another unfinished cross is known as the East Cross and has particular interest as it shows a cross in course of construction. Several blank panels are marked out for the sculptor's chisel.

Close by in the lane beside the church is St. Columb's (or Colmcille's) House, a twelfth-century stone-roofed oratory, similar in construction to St. Kevin's Church at Glendalough and St. Flannan's at Killaloe. It is small, twenty-eight feet long and twenty-one feet broad, with a steeply pitched stone roof rising to a height of thirty-eight feet at the ridge. The walls are almost four feet thick. Between the barrel vault and the roof there is a croft or apartment divided into three rooms, which may have served as dormitories for the monks. It was probably built in the ninth century by the monks who came here from Iona.

From these early Christian remains we journey to a recent development of a very different kind. On our way back to Navan we pass by the workings of Tara Mines, the largest zinc/lead mines in Europe. The workings are underground, and the buildings on the surface give little indication of the size of the undertaking. Drilling, crushing and processing are carried on well below the surface and this method of working eliminates mining noises and the creation of large amounts of waste material. Annual production of concentrates is approximately half a million tons, and the reserve consists of sixty-seven million tons of well established, indicated and potential ore. Since production began in 1977, employment in Tara Mines has grown to one thousand with a wage bill of over £20 million per annum.

This story of commercial success reminds us of the achievements of two men born in this county over two hundred years ago. In Sir Peter Warren and his nephew, Sir William Johnson, Meath gave to the world two men whose extraordinary careers seem to embody a daring and zest for life typical of the eighteenth century.

Sir Peter was born into a Catholic family at Warrenstown, within sight of the Hill of Tara, in 1703 or 1704. His father, Michael, was an officer in the army of King James II and very probably fought at the Boyne in 1690. His estates were confiscated but were restored to him under the terms of the Treaty of Limerick. Young Peter was reared as a Protestant to improve his chances, and he joined the British navy. He was helped along in his career by his relatives, Admirals Aylmer and Norris, who like himself had 'converted' from Catholicism.

He saw much service on the North American station and early in 1745 was ordered to assist in an attack on the port of Louisburg, Cape Breton Island, Nova Scotia, then in the posses-

Columba's House, Kells: an ancient oratory with a steep stone roof and early barrel vaulting. It may have been built in the ninth century by the monks who came from Iona but some authorities date it to the twelfth century.

sion of the French and the strongest fortress in North America. In the course of the engagement he captured several merchant ships with cargoes of great value. Louisburg was a port of call for French ships homeward bound from the East Indies or the Pacific. The crafty Meathman lured them into the harbour by keeping the French flag flying on the fort. One of the ships seized by this manoeuvre had money and goods on board to the value of £600,000, an enormous sum in those days. That same year, Warren was promoted rear-admiral and in 1747 he helped to defeat a French squadron off Finisterre. This service brought him his knighthood.

The navy was seen in the eighteenth century as a ready route to riches for captains who had the daring and skill to make prizes of enemy merchant ships. Sir Peter is said to have captured prizes to the total value of two million dollars. In 1731 he married Sussanah Delancey, who came from a wealthy Dutch mercantile family settled in New York. He added to his fortune by successful speculation in land and shrewd investment in trading firms, no doubt with good advice from his Dutch connections. His property included a farm of three hundred acres on Manhattan Island. It was sold by his heirs a few years after his death. Its value today would be reckoned in billions of dollars.

After the battle of Finisterre his health declined, and he left the navy to settle in London where he was MP for Westminster from 1747 to 1752. He was generally regarded as the richest commoner in the country. The family estates in Meath had been lost by his father's improvidence. Sir Peter bought them back and while on a visit to Ireland in July 1752 caught an inflammatory fever and died. There is an ornate monument to his memory in Westminster Abbey.

William Johnson was a son of Peter's sister, Anne, who married Christopher Johnson of Warrenstown. Peter brought his young nephew out to America in 1737 to oversee property he had bought in the Mohawk Valley, New York State. William became an Indian trader and by his fairness and industry won the friendship of the Indians. During the Anglo-French wars his influence prevented the 'Six Nations', the name given to the tribes of the area, from going over to the French. He was given sole management and direction of the 'Six Nations' and made a major-general in 1755. That year he defeated the French at Lake George and was rewarded with a grant of £5000 and a baronetcy. For his services against the French in Canada in 1760 he was granted 100,000 acres on the north bank of the Mohawk river. Here he built himself a new house called Johnson Hall, where he kept open house, entertaining in princely style. He induced a large number of Irishmen to settle in the district and opened it up for the development of agriculture. A contemporary described him as an uncommonly tall man with a fine countenance. His first wife died young and he then took to his house Molly Brant, sister of Joseph Brant, a Mohawk war chief, who became known as 'the Brown Lady Johnson'. In his will he styled their offspring as his 'eight natural children'. He died suddenly in July 1774 at the age of sixty-nine after delivering an address to the Indian Council of the 'Six Nations'.

Motoring into Navan, we call to mind another Meath sailor, whose name is familiar to thousands of Irish fishermen and yachtsmen, few of whom know that the Beaufort Scale of Wind Force was originated by a clergyman's son who was born in Navan in 1774.

Admiral Sir Francis Beaufort, son of the Rector of Navan, joined the East India Company at fifteen and after serving for a year in their ships, entered the British navy. It had changed little since the days of his fellow Meathman, Sir Peter Warren, and was still, in Churchill's phrase, the navy of 'rum, sodomy and the lash'. Young Beaufort took to the life, and despite the crowded squalid conditions on board a man-of-war and the complete lack of privacy, continued his study of navigation and astronomy, subjects in which he had an absorbing interest.

In 1800, as a lieutenant, he commanded the boats of the *Phaeton* in a daring exploit when they cut out the Spanish ship *San Josef* from under the guns of Fuengirola Castle, near Malaga. In boarding the Spaniard, Beaufort received sixteen slugs from a blunderbuss at point blank range, and three sword cuts. He was near to death for weeks after, but recovered to receive a dearly-bought promotion to commander. Until 1805 the Admiralty could find no ship for him, and in 1803-1804 he helped his brother-in-law, Richard Lovell Edgeworth, father of the novelist Maria, to establish a telegraph line from Dublin to Galway. In 1812 he was again badly wounded when fanatics attacked his boat's crew off the coast of Turkey.

In 1829 Beaufort was appointed hydrographer to the navy and began his real life's work. He transformed that office into the world's finest maritime surveying and chartmaking institution, and made the Admiralty Chart the model of excellence, accuracy and completeness. He was promoted rear-admiral, knighted and retained in his post until he was eighty-one. He loved his work and fretted when he retired, fearing the empty hours without employment. Despite his many wounds received on active service, he lived to be eighty-three, dying in London in 1855. His distinctions included fellowship of the Royal Society and membership of the Royal Irish Academy. When weather forecasts on radio and television refer, for instance, to winds as 'gale force eight', they are using the Beaufort Scale; he also originated a tabulated system of weather notation which is still in use.

I drive on through Navan to visit Athlumney Castle, which is only a mile or so up a side road off the main road from Navan to Drogheda. It is built on a hill at a sharp bend in the narrow road, near to a crossroads, and is surrounded by a high wall, but I was in luck as the gate was open. The castle is a public monument in the charge of the Board of Works and two men from the Board had arrived just before me. They unlocked the door to the four-storey tower and encouraged me to climb it, showing a gratifying confidence in my agility and head for heights. The ascent was not without its hazards but I was rewarded by a fine view of rich Meath pastures: Athlumney means 'the ford of the herds'. Our medieval forbears had a good appreciation of the strategic value of elevated sites and built their castles accordingly. The tower of Athlumney dates from

Top: Athlumney Castle, like most of those in the Boyne Valley, was set on a commanding eminence and there is a fine view from the top of the four-storey tower.

Rampart and old bridge, from the Lawrence Collection. This beautiful old bridge across the Boyne Canal can be reached in a few minutes from the main road outside Navan. A towpath along the river Boyne affords a delightful walk from here to Broadboyne Bridge at Stackallen.

the fifteenth century, and a Tudor mansion was added about 1600. The ruins are quite extensive and a number of mullioned windows still remain, as well as a fine oriel window in the south wall overlooking the road.

The story of the burning of Athlumney by its last lord, Sir Launcelot Dowdall, is best told in the words of Sir William Wilde:

> Sir Launcelot, hearing of the issue of the Battle of the Boyne and the fate of the monarch to whose religion and politics his family had been so long attached, and fearing the approach of the victorious English army, declared, on the news reaching him, that the Prince of Orange should never rest under his ancestral roof. The threat was carried into execution. Dowdall set fire to his castle at nightfall, and, crossing the Boyne, sat down upon its opposite bank, from whence, as tradition reports, he beheld the last timber in his noble mansion blazing and flickering in the calm summer's night, then crash amidst the smouldering ruins, and when its final eructation of smoke and flame was given forth, and the pale light of morning was stealing over that scene of desolation, with an aching and a despairing heart, he turned from the once happy scene of his youth and manhood, and, flying to the Continent, shortly after his royal master, never returned to this country.

For good measure, Sir William gives another story about Athlumney, featuring two jealous sisters, and he has relegated it to a footnote, no doubt to show that he did not entirely, or even partly, believe it:

> It is said that two sisters occupied the ancient castles of Athlumney and Blackcastle, which latter was situated on the opposite bank of the river; and the heroine of the latter, jealous of her rival in Athlumney, took the following means of being revenged. She made her enter into an agreement, that to prevent their mansions falling into the hands of Cromwell and his soldiers, they should set fire to them at the same moment, as

soon as the news of his approach reached them, and that a fire being lighted on one was to be the signal for the conflagration of the other. In the meantime the wily mistress of Blackcastle had a quantity of dry brushwood placed on one of the towers of the castle, which, upon a certain night, she lighted; and the inhabitants of Athlumney, perceiving the appointed signal, set fire to their mansion, and burned it to the ground. In the morning the deception was manifest. Athlumney was a mass of blackened, smoking ruins, while Blackcastle still reared its proud form above the woods, and still afforded shelter to its haughty mistress.

As the local saying has it, 'that's a story with a rag round it'! Navan town did not please Sir William: 'a dirty, ill-built, straggling collection of houses, boasting the honour of having been half a county town'. It is now a full county town, clean, busy and prosperous, headquarters for Meath County Council and possessing a fine county library. Like so many other Irish towns, it turns its back on its river, as Sir William complained, but the river is easily reached from the car park near the turn to Athlumney Castle. You emerge on to the ramparts, where a stretch of the canal, long disused and dry, is spanned by a beautiful old stone bridge, still in excellent repair; beyond is the river. In these few minutes you leave a busy highway and find yourself walking along a broad path in a quietness broken only by the rustling of leaves and an occasional burst of song from a blackbird or a thrush. This is surely one of the great attractions of the Boyne: its most beautiful stretches, while close to roads and towns, yet offer a tranquil solitude. From here to Broadboyne Bridge at Stackallan is the longest stretch of the canal, a distance of a little more than five miles, but as the evening is closing in, I am obliged to turn back after two miles. No matter, next week I shall be in Slane and if the weather holds, I'll walk along the Boyne from Slane Bridge to Broadboyne.

Chapter 4

Slane - Slane Castle - St. Erc - Hill of Slane -
St. Patrick - Francis Ledwidge - Walk to Broadboyne
Bridge

I have a shieling in the wood,
None knows it save my God;
An ash tree on the hither side, a hazel bush beyond,
A huge old tree encompasses it.
'King and Hermit', Kuno Meyer

As you approach Slane from the west, the road sweeps round in a wide bend and at its apex you see the entrance to Slane Castle. A short drive leads to the door of the restaurant; the night club is underneath. Like so many owners of stately houses, Lord Mountcharles has found it necessary to open Slane Castle to the public and provide guided tours, meals and other attractions to enable him to meet the costs of maintaining the establishment. Henry Mountcharles has embarked on one fund-raising enterprise which has evoked responses varying from admiration at his initiative to bitter condemnation of the resulting damage and turmoil. This is the annual rock concert, which has featured stars such as Bob Dylan, David Bowie, the Rolling Stones, Bruce Springsteen and, in 1986, the group Queen. This last group drew the biggest crowd ever, estimated at 85,000, paying £15 each which, along with sponsorship funding, yielded a total well over a million pounds. The setting for the concerts is superb; the fans assemble in the great grassy pasture land sloping down from the front of the castle to the Boyne, with the richly-wooded surrounding lands and the stately castle forming a dramatic background.

The influx of such a huge crowd, mainly under twenty-five years of age, into the village of Slane, brings problems. Experience has taught the promoters to provide large-scale security and traffic control; nevertheless, after concerts villagers have vowed 'never again will we allow this'. So far, they have been mollified sufficiently each year to allow the concerts to continue.

Slane Castle was originally the seat of the Flemings, Norman invaders who came to Ireland in 1171 and remained at Slane for five hundred years. They took the side of the Stuarts, and with the defeat of the royalist cause their estates were confiscated. The Conyngham family acquired the property and have now held it for over three hundred years. The present estate of 1000 acres includes 300 acres of woodland with some fine stands of hardwoods. The present castle incorporates part of the ancient stone fortress of the Flemings. It was rebuilt and enlarged in 1785 to the design of James Wyatt and Francis Johnston and is well worth a visit. The ballroom has a beautiful, lacy, fan-vaulted ceiling with a central pediment. Watch out for two landscapes by Thomas Roberts (1748-78): 'A View of Beauparc from the Boyne' and 'The Old Castle of Slane'.

Slane Castle, a commanding site on
the banks of the Boyne.

The Marchioness of Conyngham was the mistress of George IV of England (1762-1830) and he visited Slane in 1821. It was said that the road from Dublin to Slane was straightened to make it easier for him to see her, but as he made only one visit, this seems to be an apocryphal story. It was arranged that

Slane Castle commands a view of one of the most beautiful wooded stretches of the Boyne.

during his stay at Slane Castle the king should dine at Annesbrook, the house of a neighbouring landlord, a Mr. Smith. To make his house sufficiently grand for the occasion, Mr. Smith added a huge Ionic portico rising to the eaves, and a Gothic banqueting hall with a corridor joining it to the main house. The king was plagued with acute diarrhoea during his Irish visit. On the day in August when he went to Annesbrook the sun shone brightly; he asked that the meal be served outdoors and never set foot in the new banqueting hall. The sycophantic owner had beggared himself with this needless extravagance and was soon after declared bankrupt. As a reward, perhaps, for the tact and understanding shown by his host, then an Earl, the king made him the first Marquis Conyngham.

In the grounds of the castle are the remains of the hermitage of St. Erc, the first bishop of Slane, who was consecrated by St. Patrick and died in A.D. 514. These ruins are now completely overgrown and the beautiful pointed doorway, illustrated in Sir William Wilde's *Beauties of the Boyne and Blackwater*, has now collapsed. Sir William relates a pleasing story about St. Erc taken from a twelfth-century manuscript.

St Erc Hermitage —
this beautiful doorway
has now collapsed.

King Domhnall of Tara was preparing a great feast and sent his stewards to collect every delicacy of the season. They went forth throughout Meath in search of goose eggs and came to a small hermitage with a flock of geese at the door and inside a woman with a black hood on her head and she praying to God. They went in and found a vessel full of goose eggs. 'We have had great success,' they said, 'for should we search Erin, there could not be found more goose eggs together in one place than are here'. 'It will not be good success,' said the woman, 'and it will not redound to the happiness of the banquet to which this small quantity of provision will be brought.' 'Why so?' they said. 'It is plain,' said the woman. 'A wonder-working saint of God's people dwells here, namely, Bishop Erc of Slaine, and his custom is to remain immersed in the Boinn up to his two armpits from morning to evening, having his Psalter before him on the strand, constantly engaged in prayer, and his dinner every evening on returning hither is an egg and a half and three sprigs of the cresse of the Boinn and it behoves you not to take away from him the small store of food which he has.' But the proud people of the king made no reply to her — for they were plebeians in the shape of heroes on this occasion and they carried away the property of the righteous man and saint, in despite of her. The holy patron, Bishop Erc, came to his house in the evening and the woman told him how he was plundered. The righteous man then became wroth and cursed the banquet as bitterly as he was able to curse it.

Leaving the castle, you take the main road towards the village, which was built mainly in the last quarter of the eighteenth century under the patronage of the Conyngham family, and shows clear evidence of the planning so lacking in other Irish villages of the same size, with their monotonous, single, straggling, main street. Slane lies at the intersection of two main roads, Dublin/Derry and Drogheda/Navan, and a group of four substantial stone-built Georgian houses, one on each corner, gives dignity and spaciousness to the octagon enclosed by them. Each has two satellite houses, one on each side, and the octagon was further embellished by its street furniture of eight flambeaux, of which only the cut stone bases now remain.

An Taisce has published an attractive *Guide to Slane*, written by C.E.F. Trench, with drawings by Bea Orpen. If you can spend a day or two in Slane, this publication will help you to explore the village and its environs. Of particular value are the detailed directions for making the Boyne walk; of this, more anon.

Local memory furnished Trench with the story of the little woman who would run messages to Drogheda, nine miles distant, at a steady trot, for twopence a time; she would do that three times a day. And Trench feels for Pat McDonnell, the postman of 1913, who gave Slane four collections and four deliveries of post daily, leaving on foot at 6 a.m. for Beauparc railway station. He carried the post in to Slane at 8 a.m., set out for Beauparc again at 9 a.m. with the outward mail and returned to Slane at 10 a.m. He was on the road again at 5 p.m., back to Slane at 6 p.m., and made his final journey to Beauparc at 8 p.m., returning at 9 p.m. Official regulations forbade the use of a bicycle. And, C.E.F. Trench tells us, this remarkable man was also a butcher!

But now we must turn left at the octagon and take the road up to the Hill of Slane, where according to tradition St. Patrick lit the Paschal Fire on Easter eve. This was a violation of a law which laid it down that on pain of death no other fire should be lit in the vicinity when a great festival fire blazed on the Hill of Tara. King Laoghaire was incensed and alarmed to see this other fire and called his druids to question them about it. Their reply was not reassuring. 'If that fire which we now see be not extinguished to-night, it will never be extinguished but will overtop all our fires, and he that has kindled it will overturn thy kingdom.' The king immediately called for his chariot, set off for Slane with a small retinue and summoned the stranger to appear before him. He had ordered that no one should rise to show respect to him, but when Patrick appeared, one of the king's retinue, Erc, struck by the saint's commanding appearance, rose and saluted him. This was the same Erc whose hermitage now lies in ruins in the grounds of the castle.

The summit of the hill is easily reached through a stile and across a field towards the ruins clearly visible from the road. It is said that Erc founded a monastery there. It was rebuilt by Sir Christopher Fleming in 1512 as a monastery for Franciscan friars. A short distance away a separate building, known as The College, was built to house four priests, four lay-brothers and four choristers who would officiate at services in the church. There is a tower at the western end of the church, with a fine pointed window in the Gothic style. There is a flight of sixty-eight steps to the top of the tower. The ascent is not easy, as the spiral stairway is very narrow and some of the steps are much worn, but it is worthwhile for the active and adventurous because of the magnificent view of the Boyne Valley from the top. Sir William Wilde waxed lyrical in describing the view from the hill and the tower.

Look abroad over the wide, undulating plains of Meath, or to the green hills of Louth: where, in the broad landscapes of Britain, find we a scene more fruitful and varied, or one more full of interesting, heart-stirring associations? Climb this tower ... look from the tall pillar-like form of the Yellow Steeple at Trim, which rises in the distance, to where yon bright line marks the meeting of the sea and sky below the Maiden Tower at Drogheda ... view the hills of Skreen and Tara, pass in review the woods of Hayes, Ardmulchan, Beauparc: look down into the green mounds and broad pastures of Slane ... to where the great pyramids of western Europe, Knowth, New Grange and Dowth, rise on its left bank, see you not the groves of Townley Hall and Oldbridge, marking the battlefield of 1690 ... These steeples and turrets which rise in the lower distance were shattered by the balls of Cromwell, and that knoll which juts above them is the Mill Mount of Drogheda. What recollections gush upon us as we stand on the abbey walls of Slane, and take in this noble prospect at a glance.

The college is built around an open quadrangle, with the

The building on the Hill of Slane, which is known as the College, was erected to house
four priests, four lay brothers and four choristers who would officiate
at services in the chapel.

priests' residence on the north side. This has a number of fire-places with very large lintels. The arms of the Flemings are carved on a heraldic stone set into the west wall of the quad-rangle.

We leave the Hill of Slane and go back down to the village and down Mill Hill to the fine old bridge across the Boyne. To the left is Slane Mill, which started life as a flour and grain mill and in its day was the largest mill in Ireland. It was built in 1766 and was much admired by visitors, including Arthur Young, who described it as 'a very large and handsome edifice'. It is now owned by a subsidiary of Courtaulds and used for manufacturing cotton goods.

Near to the entrance to the mill, you will find a plaque to the memory of Francis Ledwidge, poet of Meath. It is set into the parapet of Slane Bridge and is the work of the Cork sculptor, Seamus Murphy. It bears this verse from Ledwidge's poem on the death of his friend, Thomas MacDonagh, the Easter Week leader who was executed after the Rising of 1916:

> He shall not hear the bittern cry
> In the wild sky, where he is lain,
> Nor voices of the sweeter birds
> Above the wailing of the rain.

Honour and thanks to the Slane Guild of Muintir na Tíre who had this plaque erected in 1962. We will visit Ledwidge's cottage on our way to Drogheda.

Passing over the bridge, one has a very fine view of Slane Castle and the surrounding woodlands, with a large weir in the foreground. The weir diverts water to the Slane Mill, and until quite lately some of the power for the mill was provided by this mill stream. Looking over the parapet of the bridge at the broad expanse of the Boyne, one naturally thinks of the fine salmon for which the river was famous. No longer so, alas. Fishermen from home and abroad deplore the spoiling of the fisheries by the extensive arterial drainage carried out by the Office of Public Works. The spawning beds were impacted with silt in the

Portrait of Francis Ledwidge: the Meath poet, Francis Ledwidge in the uniform of the Royal Inniskilling Fuseliers in World War 1. He survived the Gallipoli landings and bitter fighting in Serbia only to be killed near Ypres in Belgium on 31 July 1917.

Ledwidge cottage interior: the small sitting room in the labourer's cottage near Slane where poet Francis Ledwidge was born.

course of the work. Rehabilitation has been promised, but it remains just a promise.

We look over the gate at the Boyne Canal and promise ourselves that we will make the Boyne Walk some fine autumn day. It is still possible to walk from Drogheda to Navan, a distance of twenty miles, partly along the old canal towpath, partly along the river bank. But now we turn back across the bridge and up the hill to the crossroads at the octagon, pausing to admire the Gothic gate at the former main entrance to Slane Castle. This gate was designed by Francis Johnston and bears a fine stone carving of the arms of Earl Conyngham, later first Marquis, and of his wife, Elizabeth Denison. The avenue is more than a mile long and is now used only occasionally.

At the crossroads we turn right and take the road to Drogheda. About half a mile on, we come to the cottage where Francis Ledwidge was born. It was restored in 1980-81 by the Ledwidge Cottage Committee whose members, Paddy Mongey, Vivien Igoe, John Clarke, Bobby Doonan, Pearl Baxter, Joe Ledwidge (nephew of the poet) and Peter Baxter are still active with the Slane Muintir na Tíre Guild in maintaining the cottage and showing it to visitors. It is a one-storey, four-roomed structure, on the traditional cottier's half-acre of ground. Nasturtiums bloom in the small flower beds on either side of the front door. On the wall beside the door is a plaque similar to that on the Bridge of Slane. In the yard there is a small stone henhouse and pigsty. The half-acre garden where once the Ledwidges grew potatoes and cabbage is now in grass, with a half dozen trees and a few rustic seats. A large limestone rock has beside it a smaller flat stone on which are carved the lines written by Ledwidge, while he was serving as a soldier in France, in memory of Ellie Vaughey, whom he had loved and who died in childbirth, married to another:

To One Dead

A blackbird singing
On a moss-upholstered stone,
Bluebells swinging,

Shadows wildly blown,
A song in the wood,
A ship on the sea,
The song was for you
And the ship for me.

The simple and sparse furniture of the small rooms reminds
us of the truly frugal lives of cottiers and farm labourers in those
days, the dresser and the settle bed, earthenware crocks and
shining delft. The memorabilia include original letters from
Ledwidge, manuscript copies of some of his poems, and his war
medals.

He was born here on 19 August 1887, the son of an evicted
tenant. He left the local national school at the age of twelve,
and earned his living as a farm labourer and later as a road
overseer. His early poems were published in the *Drogheda
Independent*, happily still flourishing. In 1912 he sent some
verses to Lord Dunsany, who encouraged him to continue writing. He became known as a poet, but continued working as
before, became secretary of the Meath farm labourers union and
served on the Navan District Council. His love affair with Ellie
Vaughey ended abruptly and unhappily in the summer of 1913.
She was the daughter of a landowner and he was a landless
man on a poor wage. His verses over the next two years bear
evidence of the deep hurt caused to him by this rejection.

Ledwidge had organised the Irish Volunteers in Slane, but
like thousands of his fellow nationalists he joined the British
army in 1914 when World War I broke out. He served with the
Royal Inniskilling Fusiliers, and fought, he said, 'neither for a
principle nor a people nor a law, but for the fields along the
Boyne, for the birds and the blue skies over them'. The horrors
of war in Gallipoli and in the trenches of Flanders, the shock of
the news in 1915 of the sudden death of his lost love, Ellie
Vaughey, and the execution of poets Thomas MacDonagh and
Joseph Plunkett after Easter 1916, aroused in him feelings of
doubt and despair which were reflected in the poems he wrote
at that time. He mourned the leaders of the Rising:

I heard the Poor Old Woman say:
At break of day the fowler came,
And took my blackbirds from their songs
Who loved me well thro' shame and blame.

His poem on the death of Thomas MacDonagh is perhaps his best-known. We have read the first verse on the Bridge of Slane. Here are the remaining two:

Nor shall he know when loud March blows
Thro' slanting snows her fanfare shrill,
Blowing to flame the golden cup
Of many an upset daffodil.

But when the Dark Cow leaves the moor,
And pastures poor with greedy weeds,
Perhaps he'll hear her low at morn,
Lifting her horn in pleasant meads.

Ledwidge had a short leave home in May 1916, and on his way to Richmond Barracks in Dublin to report back for duty, he saw the ruins of O'Connell Street after the Rising. The British officer to whom he reported made a scornful remark about 'the rebels', to which Ledwidge replied that when he fought on two battlefields for England he had, like a fool, believed he was fighting for Ireland too.

His first collection of poems, *Songs from the Fields*, was published in 1916. In a letter from France to Katherine Tynan, who had sent him a copy of her review, he wrote: 'Death is as interesting to me as life. I have seen so much of it, from Suvla to Serbia and now in France. I am always homesick. I hear the roads calling, and the hills, and the rivers wondering where I am.'

He did not live long after his fellow-poets. He survived the Gallipoli landings and the bitter fighting that followed in Serbia, but was killed near Ypres in Belgium on 31 July 1917.

Standing outside his cottage, we recall his lines on a June day in Meath:

> Broom out the floor now, lay the fender by,
> And plant this bee-sucked bough of woodbine there,
> And let the window down. The butterfly
> Floats in upon the sunbeam, and the fair
> Tanned face of June, the nomad gypsy, laughs
> Above her widespread wares ...
> The cuckoo's voice is hoarse and broke with joy,
> And on the lowland crops the crows make raid,
> Nor fear the clappers of the farmer's boy,
> Who sleeps, like drunken Noah, in the shade.

And then the elegiac note:

> Ay soon the swallows will be flying south,
> The wind wheel north to gather in the snow,
> Even the roses spilt on youth's red mouth
> Will soon blow down the road all roses go.

Monaghan has its Patrick Kavanagh and Meath has Ledwidge. Wasteful war ended his life before his thirtieth year had begun, and before the promise of these early poems could be brought to fulfilment. But Meath remembers and honours him.

A few months later, on a sudden impulse, I resolve to go to Slane again and walk up the river bank to Broadboyne Bridge, before the late autumn days grow too short and cold. A fine October day dawns bright and inviting and I reach Slane Bridge by eleven o 'clock. On the Drogheda side a gang of young men is busy working on the canal, here badly silted up, and they tell me that the local Community Council have embarked on a project in partnership with the Inland Waterways Council to rebuild the canal walls and clean out the canal. I ask their foreman whether they mean to use heavy machinery, JCBs or the like, to excavate the canal and he shakes his head. 'Pick and shovel, Armstrong's patent,' he says, flexing his arms with a grin. 'Those machines would rip up the bottom of the canal where brushwood was laid as a foundation. It'll be slow work, very slow, but we'll have to put up with that.' He looks down-river appreciatively. 'It's a lovely stretch, there.'

I cross to the other side of the bridge and pass through a stile on to the bank of the canal. It bends round to the right to join the river a couple of hundred years further on. A concrete wall now replaces the gates of the lock which led into the river at this point. I cross over by this wall and come to a towpath along the river bank. Rushes grow thickly along the edge and I am startled when, with a loud flapping of wings, a pheasant rises suddenly from a clump and lumbers across to the opposite side. I walk on for a good half-mile, and now the river curves round to the left and the village of Slane is no longer in view. The opposite bank is heavily wooded with fine beech and chestnut trees seeming to rise from the water's edge, save where Slane Castle stands foursquare above wide green fields sloping down to the river. It is very quiet. The Boyne glides past noiselessly. There is no other living person to be seen, nor any object or building except the centuries-old castle. At this place Sir William Wilde was moved to write, 'An air of calm repose pervades this spot; the very songsters of the grove seem hushed in admiration and unwilling to disturb the peaceful thoughts which here gradually steal over the beholder.'

I walk slowly along the towpath and in half an hour come to another bend where the ground on the left rises steeply to form a rocky escarpment almost overhanging the path. This is the Maiden Rock or Lovers' Leap, in local legend the silent witness to a tragic end to young love. Past this headland the path leads to another lock, where I cross over the canal and through a gate to the grounds of Beauparc House. The path here is overgrown with long grass and passes between young trees and dense undergrowth. I have gone only a few yards when a brace of pheasant rocket up almost from under my feet and fly angrily and noisily across the river. The undergrowth seems alive with

River at Slane with boats. This photograph from the Lawrence Collection conveys the leisured atmosphere of the early 1900s as a dozen onlookers watch pleasure steamers being prepared to take passengers on a trip on 'the pleasant Boyne'.

these game birds. Some scuttle deeper into cover, a few run along the path in front of me and others take wing clamorously. I had not seen so many of them so close before in the wild state, nor realised quite how large and highly coloured they are, especially the male with his glossy dark-green head, scarlet wattles around the eyes and long pointed tail. The female, like most females in nature, wears a more sober aspect, mottled buff and blackish and with a shorter tail. And they *are* big birds, the male measuring up to thirty-five inches from head to tail, the female about ten inches shorter. I could not see them until they broke cover, for their protective colouring enables them to melt into the undergrowth and the long grass.

In some places trees have been blown down across the path but a section has been sawn out of the trunks to make a passage. I now force my way under overhanging branches and the river is hidden from view for a while. I emerge into a clearing to a view of the wide and graceful arc of Carrickdexter Weir. The Boyne seems very broad here and there is only a low murmur to be heard from the stream, flowing like a sheet of silk across the weir on the far side. I wonder how old the weir is; it probably belonged to the lord of Castledexter and the story goes that a wire was stretched from a salmon trap there to a bell in the castle kitchen. When a salmon was caught in the trap it would strike the wire in its struggle and ring the bell so that the fish came river-fresh to the banqueting table. Weirs were included in medieval times in the property registers of monasteries, and Carrickdexter Weir is surely a thousand years old. The castle itself lies in ruins, buried among the trees on the far bank. I stand looking across at the weir, reluctant to move on, the wide sweep of water, the majestic curve of the weir and the deep quiet combining to enchant the mind and senses.

A movement in the bushes calls me back from this dreamlike state and I see two men approaching, wearing dungarees and wellington boots. They are workmen from the Beauparc estate. We stand and talk; nobody is in any hurry. 'They say that the river is seventy-five feet deep, over there by the weir.' I tell them I'm making for Broadboyne Bridge, about two miles further on.

Maiden Rock, from the Lawrence Collection. One of the most beautiful stretches of the Boyne with wooded banks rising almost from the water's edge. A trip on a river steamer was an ideal way to view the scenery.

'The path is very overgrown in parts,' one of them says, 'and swampy at times after the wet weather these past months. The big storm' — he referred to Hurricane Charlie (1986) — 'knocked trees as well. You'd best go up by Beauparc House and then through the woods.' 'Yes,' they agreed, 'you can make your way along the river bank most times to Broadboyne but you'd be better off through the woods today.' They talked about the old days when river steamers, like the *Rosnaree,* brought people from Navan and Drogheda on excursions to Carrickdexter and to Newgrange. 'People don't come here anymore,' said one. 'It's a great pity; they miss a lot, flying up and down the roads.' 'They are working on the canal at Slane Bridge,' I offered. 'If the canal was opened up again all the way from Drogheda to Navan it would be used, surely.' 'Aye,' they laughed, 'maybe we'll live to see the day.' 'Will it be all right for me to go through Beauparc woods?' I ask. 'Of course. It's lately passed from the Lambarts to Mountcharles of Slane Castle. There's nobody living in the house. It's full of workmen, refurbishing and decorating.'

I say goodbye to them and scramble up a steep path to Beauparc House, built on a commanding eminence above the river. I emerge on a wide, gravelled space to find piles of rubble and planks, cars and vans and a dozen or so young men enjoying their lunchtime break in the sunshine. The house reminds me of Newbury Hall, where I began this exploration of the Boyne, as well it might, for they were designed by the same architect Nathaniel Clements, and each has a centre block with a pavilion on either side. The site was well chosen to give a view of the Boyne at its most picturesque, winding between wooded banks. I walk on down the drive and into the woods, but after a few hundred yards I find my way blocked by fallen trees, legacies of Hurricane Charlie, and decide to return to the house and make my way to the high road. It is longer than I expected to the gates of Beauparc but I press on, reflecting that before the motor car visitors to Slane came from Dublin by rail, alighted at Beauparc station and walked through the estate and along the path the way I had just come. I turn right at the gates and head for the Broadboyne Bridge. It is only a little over two

Excursions on the Boyne were very popular in the early 1900s. This photograph from the Lawrence Collection shows the river steamer *Ros na Ríghe* moored by the river bank with Beauparc House on the hill in the background.

miles but seems longer, walking on the highway, with occasional cars and vans speeding by. When I reach the bridge it becomes clear how it got its name, for the Boyne is certainly the broad Boyne here; it is also called, somewhat confusingly, Stackallan Bridge, from the name of the district. In former times when a pattern (a traditional local religious ritual) was held here it was the custom for the people to swim their cattle across the river as a charm against fairies and to ward off disease. Through a gate on the Navan side I go down to the grassy bank of the canal now completely silted up, and open my lunch basket. The bridge is a fine old structure, its semi-circular arches divided by buttresses stretching from the base to the top of the parapet. The dry canal is a melancholy sight. Would it cost so much to clean it? What an amenity it would be. But at least a start has been made four miles below at Slane — and who knows? Lunch over, I cross the bridge, walk about a mile to the main Navan/Slane road and wait for the bus, but before it comes a young man in a van stops and offers me a lift which I accept gratefully. He drops me at the entrance to the village and so I complete my day's footslogging with a last half-mile back through the octagon, down the hill and across the bridge to where I had left my car that morning.

A truism, yes, a cliché, of course, but walking is the best, if not the only, way to see and enjoy the countryside. You cannot hurry and you find yourself with time to stand and stare. The drive back to Dublin was a chore, and nothing more.

Chapter 5

Brú na Bóinne - Newgrange - Knowth - Dowth -
House of Cletty - John Boyle O'Reilly

Dead Cormac on his bier they laid:-
'He reigned a king for forty years,
And shame it were,' his captains said,
'He lay not with his royal peers.'

His grandsire, Hundred-Battle, sleeps
Serene in Brugh: and, all around
Dead kings in stone sepulchral keeps
Protect the sacred burial ground.

Just below Slane the Boyne sweeps round in a great bend, enclosing a royal necropolis, a city of the dead. In ancient manuscripts and in the oral tradition, this place is called Brú na Bóinne, 'the palace of the Boyne'. In this semi-circle of broad green fields, two miles across, are found the great Neolithic passage graves of Newgrange, Knowth and Dowth. These are megalithic monuments, that is, they are constructed from large stones, many weighing more than ten tons. There are upwards of forty round mounds in all in this prehistoric cemetery.

The first question that comes to one's mind is: How old are these tombs? And then one asks: Who built them and for what purpose? As to their age, modern techniques of radiocarbon analysis enable scientists to give approximate dates to remains, whether human or artefact. All organic material contains carbon of which a known proportion is radioactive. After death, or in the case of pottery after firing, no new carbon is absorbed by the material and the radioactive carbon already present decays at a reasonably constant rate, which can be measured. The

Above: A view of the great burial mound at Newgrange as it appeared before excavation and reconstruction. See present appearance below.

Below: Exterior view of Newgrange. The five-thousand-year-old passage grave at Newgrange is a monument considerably older than Stonehenge or the Pyramids. The clearly visible white quartz retaining wall has aroused considerable controversy since it was constructed some years ago by Professor O'Kelly.

scientist then determines the amount of radioactive carbon still present in these remains and from this information calculates how much time has passed since the death of the organism or the firing of the pottery. Other methods of dating include thermoluminescence and fission track measurements. It must be stressed that these methods yield only approximations; nevertheless, scientists and archaeologists have come to the conclusion that these tombs are almost a millennium older than was first thought, and they now place them at around 3000 B.C., making them at least five thousand years old, older than Stonehenge and older by several centuries than the pyramids of Egypt. Newgrange has been described as a cathedral of the megalithic religion. George Petrie, nineteenth-century antiquary, painter and musician, supported the claim of Newgrange to prehistoric antiquity, so as 'to allow the ancient Irish the honour of erecting a work of such vast labour and grandeur'.

And who were these 'ancient Irish', and for what purpose did they build? They were Stone Age people, who lived in substantial rectangular and circular wooden buildings. They used polished stone axes to clear the primeval forest, planted wheat and barley, and raised cattle, sheep and goats. They belonged to the Neolithic or New Stone Age.

There is no evidence that Paleolithic (Old Stone Age) man ever came to Ireland. The earliest inhabitants were Mesolithic (Middle Stone Age) people, who probably came over from Scotland about 6000 B.C. and made their largest settlements at Larne in County Antrim, where great quantities of flint were available. This material was as essential to these Middle Stone Age settlers as oil has become to their present-day successors. They were hunters and fishers, and from the flint they fashioned axes and smaller tools. Great quantities of these tools, along with heaps of shells from oysters and mussels, have been found along the Antrim coast but no trace survives of their houses or monuments.

The Neolithic people seem to have come over from Europe some time before 4000 B.C. They evidently devoted a great deal of their time and energy to the building of megalithic tombs.

Over a thousand of these have survived the passage of four or five thousand years, and it is safe to assume that many more were built and have disappeared. The different forms of these tombs, such as cairns, portal dolmens and passage graves, suggest that they were built by successive waves of settlers from abroad. These people can be called the first farmers in Ireland. In their comparatively settled way of life they acquired the arts of pottery making and weaving of textiles. It appears that they did not build their tombs until some centuries after their arrival in Ireland.

The earliest were the court tombs, so called because they included an open space or court leading into the gallery. There were many variations of this basic plan. Court tombs are found north of a line from Dundalk Bay to Galway Bay only. Pottery and flint arrowheads have been found in them, along with the ashes of the dead. Cremation was the normal method of burial, and the tombs usually faced east. Their origin and development are still a matter for debate; it seems clear that the burial of the dead was an occasion of some importance in the life of the community.

Portal dolmens are known in folklore as the beds of Diarmuid and Gráinne, fleeing from the wrath of Fionn Mac Cumhaill. Dolmen is a Breton word meaning 'table', but in fact these are megalithic tombs consisting of three or more standing stones covered by a large capstone, which can weigh up to one hundred tons. They are found mainly in Ulster, although there are some in south Leinster and Galway. The most impressive tombs are the passage graves, of which about three hundred have been found and recorded.

It is with a degree of awe that one approaches the great mound of Newgrange, remembering that it was constructed by our ancestors five thousand years ago. It comes as a shock to one who knew it thirty years ago to see the new façade of gleaming white quartz on each side of the entrance. The mound is built on a low hill about half a mile from the sweep of the Boyne to the south, hence its name in the ancient tales, Brú na Bóinne, 'the palace of the Boyne', residence of Aengus, the great god of love. It is nearly forty feet high and about three hundred feet in diameter. It contains some 200,000 tons of earth and stone and must have required the labour of many hundreds of workers — they have been described as the first wage-earners in Ireland who would have had no time to work their land. Payment would have been in kind, no doubt, although the fancy can run to visions of tokens for work done, to be exchanged for food and drink. So little is known with any degree of certainty about these builders that the temptation to let the imagination play around the subject is difficult to resist.

Walking up the hill to the mound, you first meet the survivors of a ring of pillar stones, some really enormous, which surrounded it. There are twelve left, out of an estimated thirty-five, and the sockets of some of the missing ones can be seen.

The base of the mound is supported by great kerb stones, eight to ten feet long, many bearing geometric decorations on both inside and outside faces. The stone marking the entrance to the tomb is sculptured with a triple spiral, double spirals, concentric semi-circles, and diamond-shaped motifs known as lozenges.

Newgrange — the great tumulus about 1845.

The mound is entered along a passage sixty-two feet long, lined with upright stones from five to eight feet high. The chamber at the end is circular in shape, with two side chambers and another at the end. The construction of the roof shows the skill of the builders. It rises to a height of twenty feet above the floor,

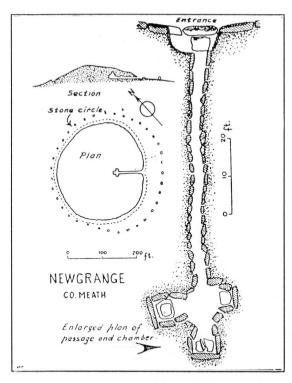

Section

Stone circle

Plan

20 ft.

10

0

100   200 ft.

NEWGRANGE
CO. MEATH

Enlarged plan of
passage and chamber

Entrance

Sunlight shining in to
Newgrange. A remarkable
feature of Newgrange passage
grave is the alignment of the
passage to the inner chambers
with the rays of the rising sun
at the solstice on 21 December.

using the technique called corbelling. Overlapping slabs were placed on top of one another until the space between the walls was spanned. Burnt soil was packed into the gaps between the slabs and this soil was the source of the radiocarbon samples used for dating the structure. One single square slab at the top closed the last space. Layers of smaller stones and water-rolled pebbles were placed between the corbels. The weight of the roof and of the cairn above it crushed these stones so as to form a bed and thus distribute the stresses evenly. The builders ensured that no water would penetrate by cutting channels in some of the roof slabs and corbels. Water filtering down through the cairn is diverted away from the chamber, which shows no sign of dampness. The side chambers contain large stone basins, one of which was carved from a block of granite from the Mourne mountains, thirty-five miles to the north-east.

The most remarkable feature of this monument is the construction of the roof-box over the entrance and its alignment with the rising of the sun on 21 December, the winter solstice. If the day is clear, the rays of the rising sun will shine through the opening in the roof-box and penetrate along the passage right into the chamber. This phenomenon was first recorded by the late Professor M.J. O'Kelly during the winter solstice of 1969.

A visit to Newgrange will make even the most prosaic of observers wish to know more about the monument itself and its builders. There has been no scarcity of comment and speculation since it was first 'discovered' in 1699 by the Welsh antiquary, Edward Llwyd. He dismissed it as 'a barbarous monument', and was equally unflattering about the entrance stone, 'a great flat stone, like a large tombstone, placed edgeways, having on the outside certain barbarous carvings, like snakes encircled, but without heads.' Sir Thomas Molyneux, professor of physic in Trinity College, Dublin, visited Newgrange about twenty years later, but he too thought little of the decorations on the stones, 'a barbarous kind of carving, showing not the least footsteps of writing.'

One who gave his imagination freer rein was Colonel Charles

Vallancey, an early member of the Royal Irish Academy. In his *Collectanea,* a series of essays published during the years 1770-1804, he advanced theories about Irish history, and Newgrange in particular, which can charitably be described as eccentric. His writings marked the origin of the 'Romantic' school of archaeology. He concluded that Newgrange was a kind of temple devoted by the Tuatha Dé Danaan to the worship of Mithras and argued that the famous carving in the chamber, sometimes called 'the ship', was in fact the name Mithras. He also propounded the derivation of the name Newgrange as 'a corruption of *Grian-uagh,* that is, the *uagh,* cave or den of Grian, i.e., Mithras or the sun.' Had he lived in the following century he might have heeded the warning of John O'Donovan, one of Ireland's greatest scholars, that the most plausible derivation of an Irish placename is sure to be wrong. It is now accepted that the name Newgrange goes back only to medieval times, when the land on which the monument stands became one of the 'new granges' of the abbey of Mellifont. Outlying farms attached to Cistercian monasteries were commonly called granges.

There is frequent mention of Brú na Bóinne in manuscripts dating from the tenth century onwards, and there can be little doubt that it had a central part in oral tradition for many centuries preceding the commitment of the legends to writing. These Boyne passage graves were particularly associated with the Tuatha Dé Danaan, people of the goddess Danu, who ruled Ireland before the coming of the Celts. Brú na Bóinne was the palace of the benevolent Dagda, his consort Boan (the river Boyne), and his son Aengus, the god of love and protector of lovers. It was sometimes called 'Caiseal Aengusa'. In the thirteenth-century *Book of Ballymote* the scribe records that 'the hoasts of great Meath are buried in the middle of the lordly-Brugh.' It was the traditional burial place for the kings of Tara.

Sir William Wilde showed more intellectual curiosity about the carvings than most of his predecessors. 'Are they mere ornamental carvings?' he asks, 'or are they inscriptions from which the history of this monument, or whatever it was originally for, might be learned? Are they ideographical or hierographic in the strict sense of that word; that is, sacred carvings? To the latter, we are inclined.'

Professor M.J. O'Kelly of University College Cork spent fourteen years excavating and reconstructing Newgrange and in 1982 published a very full account of the undertaking in his book *Newgrange: Archaeology, Art and Legend.*

Some commentators were dismayed when they saw the white quartz wall which he caused to be erected on both sides of the entrance. They thought it looked modern, and preferred the appearance of the mound when to their eyes it looked romantic and had an air of antiquity. Professor O'Kelly defended his work vigorously and asserted that Newgrange now looks as it did when first built. In the course of his excavation he found around the base quantities of quartz which had evidently fallen down from the sides of the mound. Some of this material was used by him to build a retaining wall or revêtment along a section near the entrance. Among this quartz were found boulders of granite, oval in shape and somewhat smaller than a football. These were interspersed with the quartz in the wall. The wall was then caused to collapse and the resulting stratification was compared with the original condition. It was found to correspond very closely and in some places was almost identical.

This encouraged Professor O'Kelly to proceed with his reconstruction. In his opinion, before his work Newgrange had had an appearance of abandonment and decay, with the top of the mound covered with scrub and stunted trees. When first built, it had a surface of naked stones. His critics were not mollified and one writer stated bluntly that much of the authenticity and atmosphere of Newgrange had been destroyed and that the restoration was based more on surmise than precise knowledge. The quartz must have come from the Wicklow mountains and the granite from the Mourne mountains, which are the nearest sources of these materials. Did Professor O'Kelly venture too far in accepting that they were quarried and brought to the site for no other purpose than to make the wall, now so visible? No one, or very few, will dispute that one of the motives of the builders was a desire to impress. A striking passage from a medieval

The carved entrance stone at Newgrange. The central vertical line is aligned to the rising sun at the winter solstice which shines through the opening above the entrance.

manuscript is translated as follows by Standish Hayes O'Grady in *Silva Gadelica:* 'Ireland's three undeniable eminences, dumha na ngeall, the Mound of the Hostages in Tara, Mac an Og's brugh [i.e. Newgrange], brilliant to approach and Crimthann's dun on Edar.' 'Brilliant to approach' — the very size and situation of the monument suggest strongly that it was not intended solely or merely as a tomb. And so the argument rages.

The mystery of the rock carvings remains unsolved, but speculation, informed or otherwise, has widened considerably since they were dismissed by Llwyd as barbarous. Some commentators believe that they are merely ornamental; others consider that they must constitute some kind of writing. Modern authorities incline strongly to the view that the designs must have symbolic significance, but they stop short of ascribing a meaning to them. One thing is certain: these carved stones have a haunting beauty that could not be the work of barbarians.

The ornamentation is abstract and geometrical. The designs consist of chevrons, spirals, lozenges, circles, arcs and lines. The workmanship on those slabs which are hidden behind others is inferior and suggests that they were entrusted to apprentices or perhaps to less skilled workmen. The fine craftmanship of the superb entrance stone and of the kerbstones indicates that this work was carried out by highly-skilled masters.

The most daring and imaginative attempt to solve the mystery of these carvings has been made by an American scholar, Martin Brennan. In *The Boyne Valley Vision* (1980), he sets out his conclusions from two and a half years of research. They are that at a very early date Neolithic geometers in the Boyne Valley had fully worked out the application of the geometry of the circle and the sphere to solving astronomical problems; that the stones are the repository of an entire cosmology, a vocabulary of symbols, the sun dial, the calendar and other scientific tools of this, the oldest culture known to us in Ireland. His study included the carvings found at Knowth and Dowth. Neither of these mounds is open to the public at present because longterm excavations are in progress at both.

Professor George Eogan, who is directing the work at

Above: One of the large stones called kerbstones which were found around the base of the mound at Newgrange. There were ninety-two in all and twelve, like that illustrated, were carved with intricate designs.
Below: The central cavern, Newgrange.

Knowth, has recently published an absorbing account of his investigations to date, with particularly fine photographs. He has discovered two passage tombs in the mound, one facing east and the other west. Excavating was begun more than twenty years ago, and it will probably need another five years to be completed. This may seem inordinately long, but it must be remembered that the work by its nature must be confined to the summer months, and that a wet summer can cause vexatious delays, as an open wet site makes for extremely difficult working conditions. Great care is required to avoid the slightest damage to the monument or any artefacts that may be found there.

The excitement of the discovery of the tombs is well conveyed in Professor Eogan's account. The very size of the monument and of the great stones used in its building have drawn from him the observation that such constructions demanded extraordinary commitment from what must have been an imaginative, intelligent and inventive people. Five thousand years ago neither cart-horses nor wheeled transport were available in Ireland. The stones, weighing four tons or more, were dragged a distance of several miles from the quarry to the site on wooden rollers or sledges, or simply dragged along the ground, using ropes made from twisted or plaited hide thongs. It has been estimated that it would take eighty men up to four days to bring a four-ton stone to Knowth from a quarry three kilometres distant. About 1600 stones, ranging in weight from one to several tons, were used in the making of the tomb. These Neolithic people built their houses of wood, and a good deal of timber must have been used in making the tomb, apart from rollers, sledges and levers, but no trace remains of this material.

The most striking of the grave goods found at Knowth is a decorated mace head, three inches high, fashioned from flint. The main motif on one side has the appearance of a stylised human head. Great skill and patience were required from the craftsman/artist in shaping the artefact and then working the relief ornamentation, using only a stone tool. This is just one example of the art found there, which is so profuse that Professor Eogan declares that Knowth possesses Europe's greatest

Knowth during excavation. This photograph shows the extent of the work involved in excavating a great tumulus and the care that must be exercised at every stage.

concentration of megalithic art. This art, found mainly on the lintels, corbels, kerbs and other great stones which form part of the structure, consists of geometric and other abstract motifs. Its non-representational character makes it more difficult to assign a purpose to it with certainty, but most commentators now ascribe a form of religious symbolism to these designs. Knowth is particularly rich in decorated stones, possessing about one hundred more than are in all the other tombs in Brú na Bóinne put together.

As these excavations proceed and more is learned about the people, an increase in knowledge brings with it an increase in speculation. Following his detailed description of the tombs, Professor Eogan is moved to write: 'A splendid and infinitely great monument like Knowth was probably intended as more than just a tribute to the dead. It could have been a receptacle or treasury for the emotions, feelings and thoughts of the clan, while its building was perhaps an act of faith in the future and in the continuation or prolongation of that society.' And again he writes: 'For the late Stone Age, Knowth was one of Europe's greatest public buildings. To describe it as a massive and majestic megalithic masterpiece that reflected the pride and pomp of contemporary society is not an exaggeration.' And this at once leads us to ask: What happened to this society, this living society that created a monument that has endured for five thousand years? It cannot have been a natural disaster, a tidal wave or earthquake that destroyed it, for the tomb could not have survived such a catastrophe. The dying-out of that society is as great a mystery as its beginning. But then, many civilisations have blazed like stars in the firmament, and then collapsed, leaving ruined temples, palaces and tombs to inspire moralising texts in later generations.

Work is still proceeding at Dowth, but from excavations to date it appears that this is not as fine a monument as its neighbours, Newgrange and Knowth. It is one of the earliest passage tombs in Ireland and the decoration is inferior; this prehistoric art seems to have reached its finest flowering in the adjacent tombs. Newgrange is the only one of the three open to the public

Above: An old engraving of the entrance
to Dowth passage grave.
Below: The mound at Dowth as it appeared
before the work of excavation
was begun.

as yet; Professor Eogan's book makes one look forward eagerly to the day when Knowth may be visited. Certainly it is the experience of a lifetime to stand in the inner chamber at Newgrange on the winter solstice and see the rays of the rising sun striking through the opening above the entrance with majestic accuracy, advancing down the passage, and reaching sixty feet right into the far recess of the chamber. The symbolism of the great monument seems to be embodied in this light, a message of hope and spiritual renewal. And, indeed, in 1987 the government approved a proposal to create a National Archaeological Park in the Boyne Valley on a seven-hundred-acre site embracing the megalithic tombs at Newgrange, Knowth and Dowth.

At Rossaree, on elevated ground on the south bank of the Boyne looking across to the tumulus of Newgrange, the past can seem as vividly alive as it was in the days of King Cormac Mac Airt. Cormac was renowned for many virtues and particularly for wisdom. His instructions to his son Cairbre come down to us in a ninth-century manuscript. He counsels Cairbre on bodily health, warning him against sitting too long, lifting heavy things, drying oneself by a fire and, oddly enough, sleeping with one leg over the bed rail. Cormac's death took place, according to the *Annals of the Four Masters*, in the year A.D. 266, 'at Cleiteach, the bone of a salmon sticking in his throat, on account of the Siabhradh which Malgeen, the Druid, had incited at him after Cormac had turned against the Druids, on account of his adoration of God in preference to them.' The Siabhradh were evil spirits attendant upon the Tuatha Dé Danaan, the early prehistoric gods.

Cormac had ordered his people to bury him, not at Brú na Bóinne, because it was a pagan cemetery, but at Rossnaree, and face him to the rising sun. Sir Samuel Ferguson wrote a spirited poem on this event. Against his wishes Cormac's warriors declared:

In Brugh of Boyne shall be his grave
And not in noteless Rossnaree.

But when they tried to carry his bier across the river, the

Boyne suddenly rose in flood 'and proudly bore away the King.' The bier came to rest at Rossnaree and here Cormac was buried.

He had lived at Cletty after giving up his kingship because of losing an eye in battle, a disfigurement barring him from office. But neither his grave nor the site of the house at Cletty has been identified. There are tantalising references to Cletty in the *Yellow Book of Lecan*. 'Good indeed was the situation of that house over the margin of the salmonfull, ever beautiful Boyne, and over the verge of the green-topped Brugh.'

The last king to live in Cletty was Muirchertach Mac Erca, who flourished at the beginning of the sixth century, and the *Yellow Book* includes the story of his infatuation with Sín (pronounced 'Sheen') and his death in Cletty. It is a story of love, jealousy and revenge.

The king came forth one day to hunt on the border of the Brugh and his hunting companions left him alone on his hunting mound. He had not been long there when he saw a solitary damsel, beautifully formed ... sitting near him, and it seemed to him that of womankind he had never before beheld her equal in beauty and refinement. So that all his body and his nature was filled with love for her, for gazing at her it seemed to him that he would give the whole of Ireland for one night's loan of her, so utterly did he love her at sight. And he welcomed her as if she were known to him and he asked tidings of her. 'I will tell thee,' she said. 'I am the darling of Muirchertach, son of Erc, King of Erin, and to seek him I came here.' 'Wilt thou come with me, O Damsel,' asks Muirchertach. 'I would go,' she answers, 'provided my guerdon is good.' 'I will give thee power over me,' says the king. She uttered the stave:

'There is power that is opportune
But for the teachings of the clerics.'

'I will give thee a hundred of every herd and a hundred drinking horns and a hundred rings of gold, and every other night in the House of Cletech.' 'No,' said the damsel. 'Not so shall it be. But my name must never be uttered by thee and Duailtech, the mother of thy children, must not be in my sight and the clerics must never enter the house I am in.' 'All this shalt thou have,' says the king, 'for I pledged my word, but it were easier for me to give you the half of Ireland.' She told him her name, Sín [Sheen]. They went to the House of Cletty above the brink of the salmonfull, ever beautiful Boyne and over the border of the green topped Brugh. Sín demanded that Duailtech and her children go forth from the house. Duailtech went to seek her soul-friend, the holy bishop Cairnech, who came to Cletech and cursed it and made a grave for the king.

The king sits on his throne and Sín sits on his right and never on earth has there come a woman better than she in shape and appearance. When the king looked on her, he was seeking knowledge and asking questions of her, for it seemed to him that she was a goddess of great power. He asks her, 'Tell me, thou ready damsel, believest thou in the God of the clerics, or from whom thou hast sprung in this world, tell us thy origin.' The damsel answers:

'Never believe the clerics
For they chant nothing save unreason
Follow not their unmelodious stave
Cleave not to the clerics of churches
If thou desirest life without treachery
Better am I as a friend here
Let not repentance come to thee.'

And he replies:

'I will be always along with thee
O fair damsel without evil plight
Likelier to me is thy countenance
Than the churches of the clerics.'

Proudly she relates her magic powers:

'I could create men fiercely fighting in conflict,
I could make wine — no falsehood — of the Boyne.'

In this manner she beguiled his mind and came between him
and the teachings of the clerics. But in the end they triumphed
over her magic and the king repented.

The annalist writes that Sín was a concubine, who having
lost her father, mother, sister and others of her family by the
hand of Muirchertach at the Battle of Ath Síghe (now Assey) on
the Boyne, threw herself in his way and became his mistress
for the purpose of wreaking vengeance on him. After he had
repented, she burnt the House of Cletty over his head and when,
scorched by the flames, he plunged into a puncheon of wine, he
was suffocated and so was both drowned and burned. His queen,
Duailtech, died of grief for her husband. Sín, too, died through
remorse and love for the man she had maddened by her
enchantments and then murdered.

That was the end of the House of Cletty, one-time residence
of kings. The heights above Rossnaree appeal as the likely site:
Cormac's bier was carried from Cletty to a ford and there is a
ford at Rossnaree where the Williamites crossed at the Battle
of the Boyne. The river rose and carried the bier to Rossnaree.
When Cúchulainn went a-wooing Emer, the Táin relates that
he crossed the Boann river at a ford below the House of Cletty.
There is a small mound nearby, which was sometimes pointed
out as Cormac's grave; perhaps the druids forbade his burial in
a mound more suitable for a great king. Thin evidence, for there
is more than one ford across the Boyne between Oldbridge and
Trim, and there must have been more than one *brú* or mansion
along the banks of the river. But the name Rossnaree, 'wooded
headland of kings', and the proximity to Newgrange, greatest
brú of all, makes this a fitting stage for the tragedy of Muirchertach.

A few hundred yards past Dowth mound and passage grave,
there is a roadside signpost to the Boyle O'Reilly monument. I

crossed a field and saw before me a large red-brick Victorian building and to the right the ruins of a church. In the adjoining graveyard the monument to John Boyle O'Reilly cannot be missed. It consists of a large tombstone surmounted by a Celtic cross. The tombstone bears an inscription in Irish and English above a sculptured head of O'Reilly, with attendant maidens on either side. An Irish wolfhound and a harp complete the traditional emblems. In a word, it is a conventional tombstone, larger and more ornamental than most.

There was another O'Reilly memento which I looked for in vain. In November 1884, O'Reilly wrote from Boston to an Augustinian priest from Drogheda, a Father Anderson, who had recently visited him. 'I may never go to Drogheda,' he wrote,

John Boyle O'Reilly. A native of County Meath, O'Reilly was transported to Australia on conviction as a Fenian, but he escaped to America and made a name as a poet, novelist and editor of the *Boston Pilot*.

'but I send my love to the very fields and trees along the Boyne from Drogheda to Slane. Some time, for my sake, go out to Dowth, alone, and go up on the moat, and look across the Boyne, over to Rossnaree to the Hill of Tara, and turn eyes all round from Tara to New Grange and Knowth and Slane and Mellifont and Oldbridge and you will see there the pictures that I carry forever in my brain and heart — vivid as the last day I looked on them. If you go into the old church yard at Dowth, you will find my initials cut on a stone on the wall of the old church ... I should like to be buried just under that spot, and please God, perhaps I may be.'

I could find no trace of the initials and thought that perhaps they were hidden by the thick ivy that covered most of the walls of the church. On my way out, I stopped to speak to a gardener busy at a flower bed. 'No,' he said, 'that stone is gone. When the monument was put up a few years ago, a descendant of Boyle O'Reilly came from the States for the ceremony. She knew of his wish to be buried under the stone and she had it taken from the wall and brought it back with her to Boston, to put on his grave there. It used to be in the wall just where the monument is now.'

'Is that the Netterville Institute?' I asked, pointing to a red-brick building. 'Yes,' he said. 'You'll see by the plaque over the front door that it was put up in 1877 in place of the original building.' I recalled that the institute had been founded by the eccentric Viscount Netterville as an almshouse for widows and orphans and that it had included a national school, where O'Reilly's father had been master for thirty-five years. 'Is it still in use as an orphanage?' I asked. 'No,' said the gardener. 'The trustees weren't able to keep it going with the funds they had and the way the expenses were going up all the time. So they applied to the courts and got permission to sell it. It was bought by a rich American couple. They don't come over often, but they let it to groups of Buddhists, thirty or so at a time. They spend two or three weeks here, meditating and chanting a little. They're very quiet and well-behaved, no bother or harm to anyone.'

John Boyle O'Reilly would have had the same tolerant attitude, I thought. As editor of the *Boston Pilot* in the 1870s, he opposed anti-semitism and prejudice against negroes. It seemed fitting that followers of one of the oldest religions in the history of man should come here to meditate, within sight of the great prehistoric cemetery of Brú na Bóinne.

O'Reilly's name deserves to be better known. He was born in Dowth in 1844, joined the Fenians in 1863, was betrayed in

1866 and sentenced to life imprisonment. After nearly two years in English prisons he was transported to Australia. He succeeded in escaping in 1869 on a New Bedford whaler, settled in Boston and became editor of the *Boston Pilot*. Regular contributors recruited by him included T.W. Rolleston, Douglas Hyde, Lady Wilde, ('Speranze' of —the *Nation*), Katherine Tynan and W.B. Yeats. He made a name as a lecturer and writer. His novel, *The Moondyne*, based on his experiences in Australia, went into twelve editions. He died in 1890 from an accidental over-dose of a sleeping draught.

The doubts expressed in his letter to Father Anderson that he would ever again see his birthplace were well founded. In 1885, five years before his death, he was invited to speak at Ottawa on St. Patrick's Day, but the British government refused him permission to visit Canada, although the Canadian government had raised no objection. This incident made it only too plain how little chance he had of ever returning to Ireland.

Like many other poets, John Boyle O'Reilly is remembered for one poem, 'A White Rose', included by Brendan Kennelly in the *Penguin Book of Irish Verse*. Here it is:

> The red rose whispers of passion,
> And the white rose breathes of love,
> O the red rose is a falcon,
> And the white rose is a dove.
>
> But I send you a cream-white rosebud,
> With a flush on its petal tips,
> For the love that is purest and sweetest,
> Has a kiss of desire on the lips.

Chapter 6

The Battle of the Boyne

July the First at Oldbridge town,
Where was a glorious battle,
When James and William staked a crown,
And cannons they did rattle.

The site of the Battle of the Boyne is well signposted and as the
action took place in a limited area along the river and on the
Meath side of it, it is easy to follow the events of that day. It is
as well first to make a quick tour, starting with King William's
Glen, as it has been known since the 'glorious battle.' At the
head of the glen you come to the crossroads at Tullyallen, and
Townley Hall demesne lies to your left. Turning back and
descending through the winding glen, you will appreciate why
King William stationed thousands of his men there, where they
were completely hidden from the Irish who were encamped on
the opposite side of the river on the high ground around the Hill
of Donore. You cross the river by a bridge which was built long
after the battle; from this bridge you can see Grove Island and
Yellow Island downstream towards Drogheda. You head for
Donore, encountering on the way signposts showing where the
Jacobite camp was placed and the route taken by King James's
army in their retreat towards Duleek and on to Dublin. From
the top of the Hill of Donore you have a good view of the river
and of the fields where the fiercest engagements of the day took
place. A few miles westwards the Boyne makes a great loop,
enclosing the Neolithic necropolis of Newgrange, Knowth and
Dowth, before it turns northwards to the smaller bend at Oldbridge. In 1690 there was a small village at Oldbridge, but now
there are only a few scattered houses along the road.

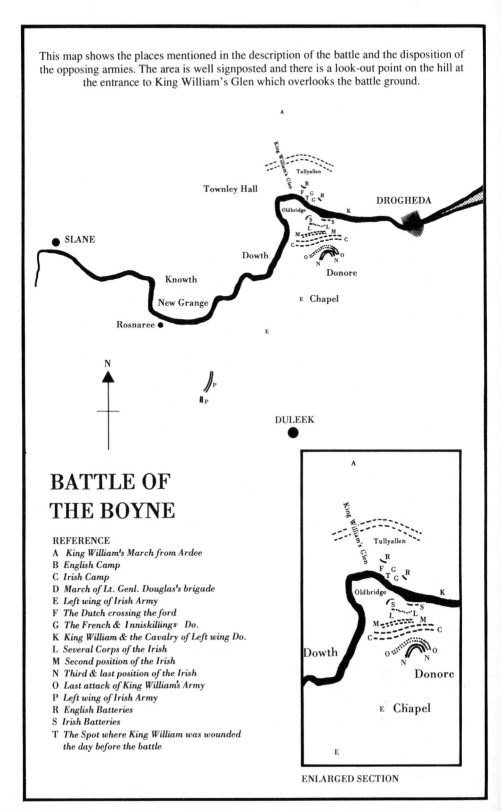

This map shows the places mentioned in the description of the battle and the disposition of the opposing armies. The area is well signposted and there is a look-out point on the hill at the entrance to King William's Glen which overlooks the battle ground.

BATTLE OF THE BOYNE

REFERENCE
A *King William's March from Ardee*
B *English Camp*
C *Irish Camp*
D *March of Lt. Genl. Douglas's brigade*
E *Left wing of Irish Army*
F *The Dutch crossing the ford*
G *The French & Inniskillings Do.*
K *King William & the Cavalry of Left wing Do.*
L *Several Corps of the Irish*
M *Second position of the Irish*
N *Third & last position of the Irish*
O *Last attack of King William's Army*
P *Left wing of Irish Army*
R *English Batteries*
S *Irish Batteries*
T *The Spot where King William was wounded the day before the battle*

ENLARGED SECTION

After this survey on the ground, the map of the battle at page 102 will become clear and the progress of the encounter can be followed without difficulty.

The protagonists were William, Prince of Orange, later William III of England, and King James II, last of the Stuart monarchy. James was the Catholic brother of Charles II, whom he had succeeded, and William was husband of James's Protestant daughter, Mary. James's policy of favouring his co-religionists aroused opposition among his English Protestant subjects, which culminated in an invitation to William to invade England and depose his father-in-law. James's support in England collapsed and he turned to Louis XIV of France for help. Ireland became a counter in the struggle for power in Europe. The Holy Roman Empire and the Catholic King of Spain were allies of William against France. Pope Innocent XI refused aid to James because of his alliance with Louis XIV. The stakes were high in the conflict at Oldbridge.

William led his army from Ardee on 30 June, and as he rode along through the rich plains of Meath he said to his officers, 'It is a country worth fighting for.' As they came to the Boyne, they could clearly see the Irish Jacobites drawn up on the slopes of Donore. The Irish cannon were placed on two elevations commanding the fords at Oldbridge. James's army was thus well placed in strong defensive positions, but was inferior in numbers to William's forces. Modern historians estimate the Irish army at 25,000 as against William's 36,000. The disparity in training and experience was even greater. Only 6,000 French on the Irish side had seen battle, whereas the Williamites included seasoned campaigners such as the famous Blue Dutch Guards, Danes, German Brandenburgers, Huguenots and British, most of those from the Continent being well-trained mercenaries. As for the two commanders, the progress of the battle showed only too clearly the difference between them.

The evening before the battle, William rode out to reconnoitre the ground. George Story, chaplain to one of his regiments, was an eye-witness.

His majesty rid on to the pass at Oldbridge...there to make his

View of Boyne at Oldbridge with obelisk. The obelisk was erected to commemorate
Schomberg and the victory of William of Orange at the Battle of the Boyne, 1690. It was
blown up by Republican forces during the Civil War.

observations on the enemies camp and positions. He and his great officers spent some time in contriving the methods of passing and the places where to plant our batteries ... Then a party of about forty horse advanced very slowly and stood upon a plowd field over against us ... they brought two field pieces amongst them, dropping them by a hedg on the plowd land undiscovered ... Their gunner fires a piece which killed us two horses and a man, about 100 yards above where the king was; but immediately comes a second, which had been almost a fatal one, for it grazed upon the bank of the river, and in the rising, slanted upon the king's right shoulder, took out a piece of his coat and tore the skin and flesh, and afterwards broke the head of a gentleman's pistol.

William shrugged off the incident. 'There was no necessity the bullet should have come nearer,' he said. But the Irish, thinking he was killed, raised a great shout, and an express was sent to Paris with the news. The guns of the Bastille were fired in triumph and the city was illuminated.

Story goes on to describe how 'at 8 or 9 o'clock at night the King called a Council of War wherein he declared that he was resolved to pass the river the next day ... One thing under consideration was how to get guides that were trusty and good. Whilst the matter was in question, my Lord George Hambleton was by, who immediately brought 4 or 5 of his Inniskilling officers that knew the fords very well and took upon them to guide the army the next day, and here it was concluded how the army should march and who should command at the different posts.'

The First of July 1690, the twelfth in our calendar, dawned bright and clear, 'as if,' says Story, 'the sun itself had a mind to see what was happening.' King William ordered his men to wear a sprig of green in their caps; the Jacobites put pieces of white paper in theirs. The Orange balladeer describes how the king led his men into battle:

> He wheeled his horse, the hautboys played,
> Drums they did beat and rattle,
> And Lille-bur-lero was the tune
> We played going down to battle.

William opened the engagement by sending 10,000 men under Lieutenant Colonel Douglas with young Count Schomberg, five miles upriver to Slane, where there was a bridge, the first after Drogheda. On the Irish side, Hamilton had advised the sending of eight regiments to protect this bridge, where there was little doubt the right wing of the enemy would attempt a passage, but King James said he would send fifty dragoons. There was a ford there also, just below the bridge. William directed that his centre, under the veteran Duke Schomberg, should cross in front of the Irish camp. He himself would lead his left wing across at a ford just below Oldbridge.

James realised his error and sent a large contingent of his army towards Slane, but the English had set out at sunrise and held the advantage. In their march they found a ford at Rosnaree, two miles below Slane, and several regiments forced their way across. They were opposed by a small Jacobite detachment, the first on the Irish side to reach the spot. After some fierce fighting the Jacobites were routed and their commander, Sir Neil O'Neill, was killed. The remainder of the Williamite army continued their march to Slane and crossed without serious opposition. They intended to press onwards and seize the pass at Duleek so as to cut off the Irish army's line of retreat to Dublin. They were foiled in this by the difficulty of the terrain, and the Irish held the pass until evening.

Shortly after ten o'clock William received a despatch informing him of the successful crossings at Rosnaree and Slane. He then ordered his army to force their way over at the fords at Oldbridge and below it. The Boyne is tidal as far as Oldbridge and the tide was out as the Blue Dutch Guards and the French Huguenots dashed into the water. It was waist-high, and they formed ten abreast with arms linked, the better to keep their footing. The river was evidently much shallower at the ford at Rosnaree, for Count de Lauzun, the French general who led the Irish there, said in his despatches that the stream was so shallow at low water that the drummers, marching across, played upon their drums without having to raise them higher than their knees.

Battle of the Boyne: a fine print of the battle showing the desperate hand-to-hand fighting of the period with William of Orange leading his troops.

At Oldbridge the Dutch and Huguenots were followed by English and Danish regiments. The Irish met them with a volley of musket fire and then charged, horse and foot, forcing some of their enemy to turn tail and rush back across the river. Most of the Williamites succeeded in gaining the far bank and here the Irish continued to charge with great spirit. Story says, 'Much about this time, there was nothing to be seen but Smoak and Dust, nor anything to be heard but one continued fire for nigh half an hour.' The Orange balladmaker's account of this crossing is so vivid that it must have been written by an eyewitness, perhaps a soldier:

> We formed our body at the ford,
> And down the brae did smatter,
> And each man grasped his fellow close,
> As we passed through the water.
> But oh my stars, had you been there,
> When we their trench came under,
> Sulphur and smoke darkened the air,
> And the elements did thunder.

And then that first repulse by the Irish:

> For man and horse fell to the ground,
> And some hung in their saddles,
> And many turned up their forked end,
> As we call 'coup the ladle'.

It was here that Duke Schomberg was killed. He had led the attack and was rallying a body of Huguenots who had been forced back by the Irish when he was struck in the neck by a musket ball. Some commentators say that in the confusion the shot came from one of his own men. He died soon after without being able to speak a word. The Reverend George Walker, hero of the siege of Derry of the previous year, was on the scene and Story recounts his fate: 'Dr. Walker, going as some say to look after the Duke, was shot a little beyond the river and stript immediately, for the Scotch-Irish that followed our camp were got through already and took off most of the plunder.' Story admired Schomberg. 'The Duke was in his 82nd year — as to his person, he was of a middle stature, well proportioned, fair complexioned, a very sound hardy man of his age. When he came to be disembowelled, his heart, entrails and Brain were as fresh and sound as if he had been but twenty.'

While the furious fighting continued at Oldbridge, with the Irish being forced back by sheer weight of numbers, King William led his left wing across at a ford nearly a mile below without meeting any great opposition. He then formed his troops to advance on the Irish flank. They retreated a short way to Donore Hill and here made a stand and drove back the Williamite cavalry. The King led a counter-charge and fierce fighting continued through the afternoon. The issue seemed doubtful for some time but, as at Oldbridge, the Irish were finally overcome by the superior numbers and equipment of the enemy and were forced to retreat. It should be noted here that besides a larger army, William had a further advantage in his artillery, which consisted of fifty to sixty large cannon and several mortars; the Irish had only twelve French field-pieces. The ballad continues triumphantly:

> Prince Eugene's regiment was the next,
> On our right hand advanced,
> Into a field of standing wheat,
> Where Irish horses pranced.
> But the brandy ran so in their heads,
> Their senses soon did scatter,
> They little thought to leave their bones
> That day at the Boyne water.

Story's version of the courage shown by the outnumbered Irish cavalry is equally partisan. 'Most of the horsemen that charged so bravely were drunk with brandy, each man that morning having received half-a-pint to his share.'

The Irish centre and right wing now fell back on the Hill of

Battle of the Boyne: a vigorous lithograph giving a panoramic view of the battle.

Donore, and as evening drew on, retreated in reasonably good order towards Duleek. Here they found the troops who had vainly tried to hold back the enemy at Rossnaree and Slane. The Williamites called off their pursuit and halted for the night. Story recounts with evident relish how his side had pursued the Irish and how they 'shot them like hares among the corn and in the hedges as they found them in their march'.

In *The Green Book*, published in 1845, John Cornelius O'Callaghan, historian of the Irish brigades in France, attacks Story's account of the battle. He says that the English army numbered 51,000 and that this figure was 'impudently reduced by Story with shameless inaccuracy and dishonesty', and that their retreat was conducted by the Irish in good order, with the Williamites showing caution in their pursuit.

The energy and courage of King William contrasts sharply with the ineptitude and indecision of King James. After issuing his orders in the morning, James retired to the little church on the top of Donore Hill and remained there for the rest of the day, taking no further part in the battle. When, in the late afternoon, he saw that the day was lost, he fled with a bodyguard of 300 horse, arriving at Dublin at nine that evening. Drogheda surrendered on honourable terms and the Jacobite garrison marched out, to join their comrades who had survived the Boyne — together to fight another day at Limerick. In fact, the Irish losses were not great, amounting to about 1300; the Williamites lost about 400. The battle was not decisive in military terms, but the psychological effect was devastating for the Stuart cause. The victory of the Prince of Orange was reported all over Europe and Te Deums were sung in the Catholic cathedrals of Austria. A tall obelisk was erected on a rock at the north bank of the river to commemorate the battle and the death of Schomberg. It was blown up by Republican forces during the Civil War in 1922. The stump and the rock are now overgrown with shrub and ivy, which hide the long inscription on the base.

Another notable name present that day was Sir Patrick Dun, after whom the former Dublin hospital was named. He was at the Boyne in his capacity as physician to the British army in

Battle of the Boyne. This fine print is in two parts. The lower part is a graphic representation of the struggle, with men and horses falling grievously wounded. The upper part shows the defeated King James taking ship for France.

Ireland, but does not seem to have left any account of his experiences.

Shooting is now prohibited in King William's Glen, which has been declared a nature sanctuary.

The old House of Lords in College Green, now part of the Bank of Ireland, has a fine tapestry depicting the battle, and there is also in the National Gallery a very large painting by Joseph Tudor (1695? - 1759) showing the obelisk with a fine view of the river as it appeared about 1746. This picture is reproduced in *The Painters of Ireland* by Anne Crookshank and the Knight of Glin (London 1978).

The 'glorious, pious and immortal memory of King William' is honoured in the North of Ireland every year on 'The Twelfth', the anniversary of the battle. Thousands of Orangemen march in procession with banners and bands through the streets of Belfast and the principal towns in a tribal ritual, seen by them as a celebration and by Nationalists as provocative triumphalism.

And now we take the road to Drogheda, leaving behind us Oldbridge and the battlefield where, in the words of Sir William Wilde, 'the sceptre passed for ever from the last monarch of the Royal line of Stuarts.'

Chapter 7

Drogheda - the Bridge of the Ford - Millmount

The most noble and wealthy city of my diocese.
Oliver Plunkett

The best way to approach Drogheda is by way of the Ramparts beside the Boyne. You can get down from the road to the riverside below Oldbridge and from there to Drogheda it is a pleasant walk, not quite two miles. The road approaches to the town, whether from the north, the south or the west, are far from impressive. Even coming along the coast road from Mornington, although one can get a good view of the Viaduct, the town itself is not seen to the best advantage. Later, we shall climb the Millmount and from that commanding height survey the town and river as they should be seen.

Now we come along the Ramparts and here the Boyne is wide and flows along smoothly past meadows and wooded heights. Nearing the town we see two fishing boats moored a few yards out in the stream. They are the traditional Spanish canoe type, with a platform at the stern to carry the net. The bow juts up to allow the canoe to be beached easily. Each boat has a crew of two, and after they have 'flaked' the net down carefully on the stern platform so that it will pay out without tangling, one man takes the rope at the end of the net and the other rows out to midstream. He paddles easily so as to keep the canoe in place, with the net stretched in a wide arc between him and the man on the shore. When they judge that the net has been out long enough, the canoe is rowed ashore and they haul in the net. Before the drainage upriver did so much damage to the fishing, there were a score or more canoes net-fishing below the Viaduct. The fishermen made their own boats and nets and before the docksheds encroached on Donors Green, they could be seen

View of the Boyne at Oldbridge. The calm rush-fringed stream,
the very spirit of tranquility.

there on summer evenings mending their nets after a day's fishing. They made their own oilskins too, from calico which they steeped in linseed oil. The fish taken in those days, in the 1920s, certainly would weigh up to thirty pounds. It is a childhood memory to see a fisherman going home along the North Strand carrying a salmon gripped by the gills, a salmon so big that its tail swished the ground as he walked along. Now there are only two canoes on the river, working the stretch along by the Ramparts.

Just above the town we get on to the main road and walk across the new bridge which allows traffic to the north to avoid the narrow bridge leading into Shop Street, itself narrow and congested. We have seen that Sir William Wilde was scathing about 'the dirt, laziness and apathy' of Trim. Drogheda fares no better. He described it as 'one of the dirtiest and most ill-ventilated towns in Ireland'. The Magdalene Tower, he said, 'is surrounded by the most wretched, miserable hovels, inhabited by the most wretched portion of the population'. We have to remind ourselves that he wrote in 1849, when the population of Ireland, in general, was probably at its lowest level of poverty, below what we now call 'subsistence level'. Earlier visitors had been much taken by the town. In the early seventeenth century, Sir William Brereton described it as the largest and best-built town in Ireland, with its houses 'fair, neat and well-built'. John Dunton, the eccentric London bookseller, visited Drogheda in 1699 and found it 'a handsome, clean, English-like town and (except for Dublin) the best I have seen in Ireland'. But a century and more of misrule and civil disorder took its toll. In a piece of purple prose, *The Parliamentary Gazeteer* of 1846 relates a story of decay. 'A huddled congeries of crooked streets — the town on the whole exhibits a strange mixture of stores and dwellings, ruins and recent architecture, woebegone lanes and cheerful thoroughfares, and may be regarded as a motley compound of the present and the past, of young expectations and extinguished hopes.'

Drogheda today (and for many years past) is busy and prosperous, and if it is not at quite such a level of well-doing as it was during the sixties, it has been less adversely affected by recent recessionary forces than, for example, Cork or Limerick.

In the mists of pre-history it is given the name of Inver Colpa, 'the Estuary of Colpa', and the district on the south side of the river just above its mouth is still known as Colpe, pronounced 'Cope'. The Irish name, Droichead Atha, 'the Bridge of the Ford', emphasises the importance of the ford across the Boyne at its narrowest tidal point. The Vikings sailed up the river and plundered the surrounding countryside. About 1172, shortly after the Norman invasion Henry II conferred on Hugh de Lacy the lordship of Meath, including 'the town of Drogheda'. Two separate towns had grown up, one on either side of the river. De Lacy received his grant for the town on the south side, and at the same time Bertram de Verdon was given possession of the town on the north side 'with the maritime lands of Louth.' Each town had its own corporation granted under royal charter. For two centuries they vied with each other until in 1412 they were united by a new charter under one corporation. The motto inscribed on the ancient armorial bearings reads 'God our Strength, Merchandise our Glory'.

Ecclesiastically, the river still forms a divide, for the northern half of the town is in the archdiocese of Armagh, and the southern Meath side is in the diocese of Meath. Schoolchildren of fifty and more years ago on the northern side complained that the catechism they had to learn by heart had much longer and more complicated answers than that of Meath, with its answers all in one short sentence each. There were splendid certainties of dogma then in the diocese of Meath. And speaking of dioceses, the boundaries of Irish dioceses were drawn so as to give each bishop direct access to the sea or to a tidal river. In those days when episcopal and temporal powers often resided in the same person, none of their lordships would tolerate being obliged to ask permission of a brother prelate to pass through his territory to make *ad limina* visits to Rome.

The town grew and prospered under its new unifying charter. The Parliament of the English Pale assembled here at least six times in the fifteenth century. The corporation was granted the right to coin its own money, and about this time, permission was given to constitute a university in the town with the same privileges as Oxford University. This project was never brought to fruition because of the lawless state of the country.

The most famous, or infamous, parliament held in Drogheda was that of 1494 which enacted Poynings' Law, named after Sir Edward Poynings, the king's deputy. This law provided that the Irish Parliament could pass no laws unless they were first approved by the king and the English Council, and it remained in force until 1782.

Another infamous date in Drogheda history is 10 September 1649, when Oliver Cromwell captured the town and put the inhabitants, men, women and children, to the sword in a fearful massacre with which his name is forever associated in folk memory. The few who escaped death were shipped as slaves to the Barbados. Remembered, too, are the words he used in reporting his victory to his masters: 'I am persuaded that this is a righteous judgment of God upon these barbarous wretches who have imbued their hands in so much innocent blood.'

But now, having crossed the Boyne by the new bridge, we turn right into narrow West Street and right again down a lane bringing us to Drogheda's oldest monastic site, St. Mary's Priory in Old Abbey Lane. The townspeople, according to tradition, founded a monastery here in the fifth century in honour of St. Patrick. The *Annals of the Four Masters* record that it was raided and burnt by the Vikings in A.D. 849. In the thirteenth century, the Augustinians founded St. Mary's on the site of the old monastery. After the dissolution of the monasteries in 1539 the property passed into lay hands. All that remains now is the central belfry tower surmounting a Gothic archway and two fragments of wall, standing forlornly in a lane of sheds and small one-storey houses.

From the remote past, we walk along West Street to visit the imposing modern Gothic style church of St. Peter, built in the 1880s. Here you may see the blackened head of St. Oliver Plunkett preserved in a shrine on a side altar, and the massive door of the cell in which he was imprisoned in Newgate Gaol in

London before his execution at Tyburn on 1 July 1681 (old style). It is secured by two huge bolts and a great padlock. The hinges measure two feet long by four inches wide. There is a small wicket door about six inches high which may have been used to push in food to the prisoner. A chilling exhibit.

On the opposite side of West Street is the White Horse Hotel, the oldest establishment of its kind in the county. It was the scene of a narrow escape by the daredevil Collier the Robber, who was a friend to the poor and often helped by them to evade the law. On this occasion he was having a meal in the White Horse when he was recognised by two men in the dining room. The servant girl saw them looking at Collier and then talking intently to each other. Suddenly one of them rose and left the room. The servant understood instantly that he had gone to inform the officers of the law. She dashed into the kitchen and returned with a bowl of cold soup which she placed in front of Collier. When he tasted it, he swore at its coldness and ordered the servant to take it away and bring him proper hot soup. The girl looked at him boldly and said in Irish, *'Má's maith leat bheith buan, caith fuar agus teith'*, which means either 'If you want to live long, eat it cold and hot' or 'If you want to live long, eat it cold and fly'. She winked at him with a half-nod at the man watching. Collier understood, leaped to his feet and made his escape.

Collier was born in Bellewstown in 1786 and died there in 1849. Despite his standing in local folklore as a hero, it seems that after capture and sentence to transportation, he turned informer and was pardoned. He lived quietly in Navan for many years after his release.

Further along West Street, at the junction with Shop Street, stands the Tholsel, a fine eighteenth-century building of local limestone, surmounted by a tower with a large four-faced clock. The corporation had its offices and council chamber there until it moved to the new courthouse in Fair Street in 1889. It is now owned by the Bank of Ireland, which maintains it in excellent condition. In the 'hungry thirties' an observant young boy noticed how the unemployed men (there were no unemployed women then!) who congregated there for company, moved with the sun from the Shop Street to the West Street frontages.

From here, the wide Laurence Street leads up a gradual slope to the massive St. Laurence's Gate, a barbican or advanced fortification outside the walls of the town, the finest of its type remaining in Ireland. It dates from the thirteenth century when the two boroughs were separately walled. The town walls were one and a half miles in circumference and enclosed an area twice that of the city of Dublin at the time. They were twenty feet high and six feet thick at the base, tapering to four feet thick at the top. Buttresses and platforms were added after the invention of gunpowder and cannon. A well-preserved portion of the wall still remains nearby on the south side of the street. Laurence Street has some excellent eighteenth-century houses. The finest two, Singleton House and Mr. Clarke's Free School, are under threat of demolition. Henry Singleton (1682-1759) was Chief Justice of the Common Pleas and Master of the Rolls, and his house, built about 1720, is a large seven-bay, three-storey brick building, with round-headed door case, parapet and cornice. The interior included some fine panelling in the staircase and in some of the rooms. All the windows were fitted with panelled window seats, as was the custom in residences of the time. It was one of the most impressive town houses in the country, outside Dublin.

The adjoining smaller house, Mr. Clarke's Free School, dates from the 1740s and replaced the old schoolhouse in which Drogheda Grammar School was established under the Erasmus Smith Endowment in 1669. Towards the end of the eighteenth century the Grammar School had taken over both houses and it remained in possession until 1977 when it moved to new premises outside the town on the Mornington road. The property has been bought by a consortium, mainly of local businessmen; they plan to demolish the houses and replace them with flats and townhouses. Local conservationists have banded themselves together in the Drogheda Grammar School Preservation Committee in an effort to save these buildings which form so integral a part of the streetscape. In the meantime,

St. Laurence's Gate, Drogheda. This thirteenth-century barbican or advance fortification with its two perfect round towers of four storeys is the finest of its type remaining in Ireland. A well-preserved portion of the old town wall complete with buttresses and embrasures survives a few yards south of the gate.

these buildings are being allowed to fall into decay and it is not possible to be hopeful about their final fate. However, the latest decision by An Bord Pleanála, while allowing the proposed development, has imposed a condition that the front and rear façades of Singleton House must be repaired and retained, giving some hope that at least the streetscape will be maintained.

We turn up Palace Street, so named because the primates of Ireland lived there in a small manse. It is a strange story. Edward I (1272-1307) decreed that no Irishman should ever be archbishop 'because they always preach against the King', and so the See of Armagh was filled by 'men of English blood or birth'. The Irish dean and chapter in Armagh refused to accept this and transferred their administration to Drogheda. St. Oliver Plunkett (1625-81) spent some of his primacy in the town which he described as 'the most noble and wealthy city of my diocese'. The Catholic primates continued to live in Drogheda until 1835. The palace or manse in Palace Street was demolished about 1800 and the primate then moved to Laurence Street.

A short way up Palace Street we turn into William Street and come to St. Peter's Church of Ireland church, which before the Reformation served as a Pro-Cathedral for the archbishops. The ecclesiastical courts of Armagh were regularly convened here, important synods were held, bishops were consecrated and priests ordained. A notable primate associated with St. Peter's was the Italian, Octavian del Palacio, who came from the Florence of Michelangelo and Bramante to rule over Armagh diocese for thirty-four years. He was buried here in 1513. In 1649 a number of the citizens sought refuge from Cromwell's soldiers in the old wooden steeple, but on the orders of the future Lord Protector himself, the steeple was set on fire and they were burned to death. Here is how Cromwell described this exploit: 'One hundred of them having taken possession of St. Peter's steeple and a round tower next to the gate, called Saint Sunday's, I ordered the steeple of Saint Peter's to be fired when one in the flames was heard to say "God confound me, I burn, I burn" ... I thank God for this great mercy vouchsafed to us.' He prayed Mr. Speaker of the House of Commons 'to remember that it is good that God alone should have all the glory'.

The present church dates from 1753; the beautiful porch and steeple, designed by Francis Johnston, were added about 1795. This splendid building, with its cut stone façade and rich rococo plasterwork, is one of the finest eighteenth-century churches in the country.

At the north-east corner of the surrounding graveyard there is a grim reminder of the Black Death, the great plague which ravaged Europe in the fourteenth century. It is a large cadaver tombstone slab imbedded in the wall. An inscription on the slab, dated to A.D. 1520 approx., states that it is of Sir Edmond Golding and his wife Elizabeth Flemying, daughter of the Baron of Slane. This is one of the few examples in Ireland of this sort of funerary sculpture, which reminds the onlooker of the mortal decay which is the fate of all, and which emerged in Europe at the time of the Black Death and persisted during the fifteenth and sixteenth centuries. Almost half the population of England died during the plague, and Ireland fared little better. It is a strange manifestation that at such a time gravestones were carved with these representations of bodily decomposition, as if the mourners needed any reminder of their own tenuous hold on life.

At the eastern end of the churchyard you may pass through a gate in the wall to see The Alleys — three terraces of small, charming early eighteenth-century houses, built as almshouses for the widows of Protestant clergy with money left by Primate Narcissus Marsh (founder of the library in Dublin which bears his name) and Primate Boulter. There are sixteen houses in all and they are all still occupied.

The main gates to St. Peter's Church are very fine examples of wrought-iron work made in Belfast, and what a pleasure it is to see how well they are maintained.

We turn north, up Magdalene Street Lower, to see Magdalene Tower, all that remains of the once great Dominican friary founded here about 1224 by Lucas de Netterville, Archbishop of Armagh, and dedicated to St. Mary Magdalene. It stands on the highest point of the northern side of the town in a small open space protected by railings. It was the belfry tower of the friary and rises two stories above a fine Gothic arch. Here King Richard II received the submission of O'Neill and the other Ulster chiefs at the end of the fourteenth century.

The English novelist, William Makepeace Thackeray, was here in 1842, not many years before Sir William Wilde. Thackeray was as horrified as Sir William at the dirt and poverty he saw in Drogheda and elsewhere in his peregrinations through Ireland, although he thought that the people were happier, though so much worse off, than the poor in England. (Did not a recent E.E.C. survey find that the Irish are the happiest people in Europe?) The Englishman knew his history, and looking at the tower he recalled how the Ulster chiefs 'flung their skenes or daggers at the feet of Richard, and knelt to him and were wonder stricken by the richness of his tents and the garments of his knights and ladies'. 'There is a beautiful old manuscript in the British Museum,' continued Thackeray, 'which shows these yellow mantled warriors riding down to the King, splendid in his forked beard, peaked shoes, embroidered gown and long dangling scolloped sleeves.' Perhaps the Ulstermen were not so impressed, after all, for their submission did not last very long. Back in Ulster they carried on in their old independent ways, and it was all to do again for another five hundred years. Thackeray cast an astringent and sceptical eye on the Irish scene, but for all his sharpness, his inability to comprehend the deviousness and subtleties of the Irish national character allows the Irish reader an occasional quiet smile.

Poor Thackeray. The cadaver tombstone upset him terribly when he visited St. Peter's, and he wrote, 'There is a hideous stone monument in the church-yard, representing two corpses half-rotted away.'

Now we make our way to Fair Street, a fine thoroughfare of late eighteenth- and early nineteenth-century houses, for many years the private residences of doctors, lawyers and other leading citizens of the town. With its mellow redbrick and attractive doors and fanlights, it reminds one of Georgian Dublin, on a smaller and more intimate scale. The chief ornament of Fair Street is without question the courthouse, built in limestone ashlar to the design of Francis Johnston. It was originally erected as a corn exchange, and on the green cupola you may see an unusual weathervane which will repay closer examination. It is a symbol of the corn trade, recalling the purpose for which the building was erected. The cock has a plough as body, a sheaf of wheat for tail feathers, a sickle for the beak and the star and crescent emblem of Drogheda for a crest.

The Fair Street Cinema, closed now for many years, stood along the opposite side from the courthouse. Here, on a Saturday afternoon, we queued for the matinee, or rather milled around in a noisy mob and rushed for the entrance when the doors opened. Those were the days of the silent films with a piano player pounding out music to harmonise, he hoped, with the goings-on above him on the screen. There was no piano player at the matinees: he would not have been heard above the whistles and shouts, 'Come on, the chap', 'Watch out behind you, mister' and so on. As well as piano playing, for big nights, like the showing of *The Prisoner of Zenda* or *The Count of Monte Cristo* or *The Covered Wagon* the adults had 'effects' from behind the screen. Thunder was simulated by shaking sheets of tin, sword fights were accompanied by 'realistic' clankings of metal bars and the Seventh U.S. Cavalry never charged the Red Indians without the accompaniment of rousing blasts on a bugle. Happy days.

We walk downhill to Shop Street and then turn left along the Mall and come to the Mayoralty House, built by the corporation in the spacious and leisurely days of the eighteenth century to accommodate municipal receptions, addresses of welcome, etc. The Freedom of the Borough was conferred here on Charles Stewart Parnell in 1894, and the Nationalists of the town subscribed £100 for a silver box for the occasion. This is a dignified building constructed with the local limestone, two storeys high, with round-headed windows on the ground floor and an elegant Venetian window on the upper storey. In the 1920s the ground floor was known as the Mayoralty Rooms and contained a reading room and a billiard room. These rooms were used as a club by the better-off townsmen. Some years ago the corporation sold the premises to local business interests. The splendid ballroom on the upper floor was then ruined by its division into storeys but fortunately the original ceiling with its Georgian plasterwork has remained intact. It must be said, too, that the new owner has restored the exterior stonework so that the long façade facing eastwards remains virtually unchanged and unspoiled.

Between the Mayoralty House and the Viaduct, the quays present the usual modern dockside vista of utilitarian sheds, warehouses and cranes. Within living memory, cargoes were unloaded using only the ship's derricks. Cattle and sheep were herded into lairages or enclosures and sometimes held there overnight before being driven up gangways into the ship's hold. There was noise and confusion, the terrified bellowing of the cattle, the shouts of the drovers and the whacks of their ashplants on the flanks of reluctant animals. Now and again a bullock would charge wildly down the quay but there were always plenty of idlers standing around to herd it back to the ship. The lairages were separated from the quays by a wide road and the road and quay soon had a liberal application of cow dung on a day of loading. Before World War I there was a thriving trade with England in live cattle and sheep; as the song had it:

> Sure the best of Welsh mutton and English roast beef,
> Came over in ships from old Ireland.

The cattle dealers, big, stout, red-faced men in frieze overcoats, embarked with their charges. The steamer, the *Mellifont* or the *Colleen Bawn*, sailed with the tide and the dealers stayed up all night in the saloon, drinking and playing cards. The attendants spoke with awe of the thick wads of banknotes flung across the tables. The cargo was unloaded at Birkenhead and the dealers went ashore to the markets. Late that evening they would straggle back on board, having been on their feet all day, bargaining, arguing and drinking. But now they would make straight for their bunks and spend the passage back to Drogheda sleeping like the dead.

Work on the quays was hard and rough and the working conditions were primitive. Unloading a coal boat was one of the worst jobs. Half-a-dozen men were stationed in the hold, shovelling the coal into ten-stone bags. These were hoisted on deck by the ship's derricks, using rope slings. Other men then lifted the bags on to their backs and ran down to the quay on a single long gangplank about two feet wide, bare of handrail, which bounced up and down with the weight of the men. They ran across the quay and the road to an open coal yard and emptied the bags there. It was dangerous and dirty work. The men in the hold were black with coal dust in a few hours. The men carrying the bags worked like coolies in the Far East; it was little better than slave labour.

More memories of life on the quays in the twenties come crowding back. The Harbour Commissioners' dredger, the *Moy*, was then moored just above the Viaduct and under its skipper, Micky Dan Mc Guirk, kept the channel swept clear. Micky Dan had a perpetual shake, head nodding in time to his arms and shoulders. The story went that he had been a deep-sea sailor in his youth and in a South American port, probably Buenos Aires or, as the sailors called it, 'Bows and Arrows', he was working aloft on a full-rigged three-master at anchor in the roads when he lost his footing and fell from the topgallant yard. He missed the deck, fortunately, went down one side of the ship, came up the other and was hauled on board. When he came to, he had the shakes. Well, shakes or no, it was a treat to see Micky Dan going aboard the *Moy*, walking up a long, narrow gangplank like those used by the coal-heavers, the plank bouncing up and down with his weight, his head and arms keeping time and Micky Dan keeping his balance as gracefully as a circus tight-rope walker. Men half his age with no disability would think twice of 'walking the plank' to board the *Moy*, and we young active boys thought it no small feat either.

Favoured ones were taken by Micky Dan on his trips down the river and out to sea, steering north to a point off Clogher

Head, where he would open the bilge doors and deposit the thick mud from the river. The spot was chosen carefully so that the tide would carry the spoil away from the coast. Sometimes Micky Dan would let one of us steer the unwieldy vessel, showing us how to watch her bow and 'give her a spoke or two now and then' so that she kept a straight course.

He lived in Baltray at the mouth of the Boyne and often walked home. A friend and neighbour gave him a lift in his Ford car one day and Micky offered to steer her so as to give his friend 'a spell'. The friend demurred; the old sailor had never driven a motor car. 'What's the difference to steering a ship?' said Micky. 'You just give her a spoke or two to keep her straight.'

Another memory. At the age of eighty-four Jack McDonnell, the Harbour Master, was still to be seen patrolling the quays on his old bicycle, directing captains new to the port to their proper berths. Someone asked, 'How does Jack keep going so fresh and well and he over eighty?' 'Well,' came the answer, 'all his life Jack's had only two speeds, Dead Slow and Stop.'

Jack McDonnell and his bicycle have long since left the scene and the port is now busier than ever, with far larger ships than those of his day lined along the quays.

That masterpiece of Victorian engineering, the Boyne Viaduct, fills the skyline as we walk down the quay. When completed in 1855, it was looked upon as one of the wonders of the age. The railway line from Dublin to Drogheda had been opened as early as 1844. The deep valley across the Boyne presented a challenge and this was taken up by a native son, Sir John Mac-Neill, who was born in Mountpleasant, County Louth, in 1793. He was a leader in his profession and a Fellow of the Royal Society. With Sir John in charge, the work began in 1851 and the project was completed triumphantly four years later. The central portion over the river has a lattice girder span of 226 feet, with a similar span of 141 feet on each side. The line is carried from the station on the south side on twelve massive limestone arches, and is continued by three more on the north side. The central span gives a clearance for shipping of ninety feet above high water. Passenger trains to Belfast proceed slowly

Drogheda Quay with sailing ships. At the turn of the century the port of Drogheda was always crowded with sailing ships. It was said that at times one could cross the river by stepping from deck to deck of these ships.

across it after leaving Drogheda station, so that the traveller gets an opportunity to survey the town spread out beneath him. The Viaduct was the locus of another engineering feat between 1930 and 1932, when it was decided to replace the wrought-iron work by steel girders so that the bridge could take heavier and faster trains. The work was carried out without any interruption in the service although traffic on the line was quite heavy in those years.

On the seaward side of the Viaduct we come to Donors Green, a favourite walking place for the townspeople on summer evenings before the motor car changed all our habits. Here we turn back and retrace our steps along the quay, making for the bridge that leads to the Meath side of the town and the Fort of Millmount. On our way we remember three natives of the town who won distinction in different callings: John Edward Healy (1872-1934), editor of *The Irish Times*; Nano Reid (1905-1981), one of Ireland's major painters; and Eliza O'Neill, Lady Becher (1791-1872), the most celebrated actress of her day.

Healy was educated at Drogheda Grammar School and Trinity College, Dublin, where he read classics and modern literature with distinction, winning many prizes. He then entered journalism, became editor of the *Dublin Daily Express*, was called to the Bar and in 1907 was appointed editor of *The Irish Times*. Sir John Mahaffy, later to become Provost, had been his tutor at Trinity and remained his friend and counsellor. Mahaffy regarded nationalism as little better than provincialism and dismissed the idea that any worthwhile literature could exist in the Irish language. In the manuscripts that had survived, he asserted, there was nothing that was not either silly or indecent when it was not merely religious. With such a mentor, it is not surprising that Healy emerged as an opponent of Irish nationalism and that he used all his influence to keep Ireland within the British Empire. Interestingly enough, Mahaffy proposed in 1917 at the Irish Convention held in Trinity College that Ireland should have a federal constitution on the model of Switzerland, with Ulster as an autonomous province. Healy remained at *The Irish Times* until his death in

Above: Drogheda in 1798. The river bank with sailing ships moored in the stream
and citizens taking the air.
Below: View of the Boyne Viaduct from below the town. This picture was taken from
Donors Green, a small park below the Viaduct, favoured by the townspeople for an
evening walk in times gone by. On the opposite bank can be seen the boathouse
of the Rowing Club. Boathouse and club are now no more.

1934 and his twenty-seven years as editor and principal leader writer made him well known in Britain.

Nano Reid was educated by the Dominican nuns at the Siena Convent in Drogheda. She won a scholarship to the Metropolitan School of Art, was a Douglas Hyde gold medalist and exhibited at the Royal Hibernian Academy for the first time at the age of twenty. At this time she painted portraits, still lifes and figure studies, but becoming dissatisfied with this narrow range, she went to Paris in 1927 with a few friends for further study. A period in London followed and then she returned to Dublin. Her reputation grew, and in 1950 she was selected with Norah McGuinness to represent Ireland at the Venice Biennale. Her work was included in the Guggenheim International Award exhibition and she was a regular exhibitor in Dublin with the Living Art group. Her pictures are on permanent exhibition at the Hugh Lane Municipal Gallery, Dublin, the Santa Barbara Art Gallery, California, and the Irish Institute, New York.

Despite these distinctions, she found it difficult to sell her paintings to make ends meet and eventually she retired to Drogheda to live with her sisters. She died in hospital here in November 1981. *The Irish Times* published this appreciation: 'She will be remembered for her poetic evocations of the Irish countryside, its people, birds and animals, and especially the remote and hilly regions of County Louth where she found her deepest inspiration.'

Eliza O'Neill was born in Drogheda, where her father was actor-manager of the local theatre, and made her first appearance on the stage there as a child. After playing for two years in Belfast, she went to Dublin and soon made her name. In 1814 she was engaged for Covent Garden. Her first appearance in the part of Juliet was a triumph and for five years she had a career of unbroken success, being particularly admired in comedy. She was looked on as a worthy successor to the great Mrs. Sarah Siddons, with less tragic intensity perhaps, but with more sweetness and charm. In 1819 she retired from the stage to marry William Becher, Irish M.P. for Mallow, where he had considerable estates. He was created a baronet in 1831. She never returned to the stage and died in Mallow in 1872. Eliza was a classical beauty, with a deep, clear and mellow voice; she was much admired by Hazlitt and her early retirement was a great loss to the theatre.

Millmount Fort towers over the town of Drogheda. It is quite a steep climb up from James Street, and if you have had enough of uphill walking through the town already, it would be as well to motor up. At the foot of the fort there is a barrack square, surrounded by eighteenth-century houses built to accommodate the British garrison of those days. An enlightened corporation has renovated several of these houses, and they are now used as craft centres. Another of them houses the Millmount Museum, founded in 1974 by the Old Drogheda Society, where I was welcomed and shown around by John Rooney of the society.

Among other items, the society has succeeded in assembling a splendid collection of banners of the guilds and trade unions and of local workers. These must have been a brave sight when they were carried in procession with, no doubt, a rousing tune from the local band to set the step and pace for the marchers. The only surviving Irish guild banners are here, those of the Drogheda Weavers and of the Drogheda Carpenters. In 1836 there were 2500 weavers in the town. Their banner measures six feet eight inches by seven feet and is painted on silk with corded silk borders and a gold fringe. It many possibly date from before the Act of Union of 1801. At the top in gold lettering is the inscription, 'We Are But One'. A queen is depicted sitting by the sea with a scroll in one hand and a shuttle in the other. The Weavers' Arms are shown in colour and below, the motto, in gold lettering on a pale blue scroll, reads 'Weave Truth With Trust.'

The Carpenters' banner, dating from the early eighteenth century, is equally fine. It is seven feet nine inches by seven feet three inches and is painted on linen with a silk border. It depicts the Carpenters' arms set in a classical doorway, with the

*Above:*Weavers' banner — one of the two surviving Irish guild banners preserved in the Millmount Museum at Drogheda. In 1836 there were 2500 weavers in the town.

Below: Banner of the Boyne Fishermen. This beautiful banner depicts a scene familiar to Drogheda people in the years before World War II when the salmon fishing flourished.

motto beneath, 'Love The Brotherhood'. The crest is an angel holding a mallet.

The banner of the Boyne Fishermen glows from the wall of an inside room. This splendid work is the masterpiece of William Reynolds (1842-81), a local painter, who also painted the banner of the Drogheda Labourers' Society displayed on the opposite wall.

Two fishermen are shown hauling in a seine net in the lower reaches of the Boyne, with the Railway Viaduct, built in 1855, and other town landmarks in the background. A third fisherman kills a salmon with a blow from a wooden club called a 'priest'. These are portraits, and the third man has been identified as the grandfather of Mrs. Moira Corcoran, a leading member of the Old Drogheda Society. This internal evidence has enabled the Society to date the banner to 1873. The fisherman in the middle is smoking a clay pipe. These were made locally and you can see one of the moulds for them in another room of the Museum.

The banner is painted in oil on canvas and measures nine feet by twelve feet. It has red, green and gold borders, poles, gilt braids, fringes and a top piece of corded silk inscribed 'Ireland For The Irish'. The back depicts St. Peter standing on a globe, pointing to the church of Rome on a rock in a stormy sea.

The banner of the Drogheda Labourers' Society is also painted in oil on canvas, with borders of two corded silks, one pink, one green, and measures nine feet by eight feet six inches. The labourers were agricultural labourers and the banner shows a man cutting corn with a sickle, attended by a woman, probably his wife, who holds a sheaf in her arms, and a child in petticoats. Above are portraits of O'Connell and Wolfe Tone, set in oval frames of ears of wheat. The back shows Adam and Eve, wearing grass skirts, being expelled from the Garden of Eden, a painting which, in its naiveté and clear, bright colours, irresistibly recalls the work of the Douanier Rousseau.

Although agricultural labourers were more numerous then than any other class of worker, they seldom formed associations or unions. Neither did the fishermen, and this lack of tradition gave Reynolds freedom to exercise his imagination in painting these banners. To this we owe the fascinating local detail in both banners and the freshness and simplicity of the compositions.

Other interesting banners displayed in this museum are those of the Boot and Shoemakers, of the Brick and Stonelayers, the Drogheda Bakers, the Drogheda Branch of the Irish National Foresters, and a temperance banner, painted in 1845, five years after Father Mathew founded a temperance branch in the town. The highly-coloured Foresters' banner shows a man in full Forester's uniform, complete with cocked hat and sword, handing a cup of tea to a man half-rising on his elbow in bed; in his other hand the Forester holds a basket of fruit for the invalid.

We turn back for another long look at the appealing banners painted by William Reynolds. Perhaps the charm of those fishermen's and labourers' banners lies in their faithful and affectionate rendering of ways of life that have gone for ever.

The items on display in the other rooms are as interesting as they are varied. An aquatint of the Phoenix Park murders stopped me in my tracks. Was this a true-to-life picture of Fitzharris the Cabman, 'Skin-the-Goat', who drove the assassins to the park that fateful day in May 1882, this merry-looking fellow with close-cropped grey hair, turning white in places, and thick moustache? On the wall nearby hang flintlocks and muskets, called 'Brown Besses', used by the town watch in the 1780s, and a flintlock found in a ditch at the site of the Battle of the Boyne.

Implements from long-vanished trades are there in plenty along with a beautiful old weighing scales in brass and iron, about three feet high, medieval coloured floor tiles found at Magdalene Tower, a heavy and threatening pair of iron manacles from Drogheda Gaol, and a well-finished coracle or round fishing boat, of the type used on the Boyne from time immemorial to within living memory. Seasoned hazel rods are used in making the coracle, with a gunwale of withes woven on to the rods. It has only one thwart or seat and is covered with oxhide, which is first softened by immersion in the river.

Boyne coracle. This round boat was in use on the Boyne down to the thirties. A fine specimen can be seen in the Millmount Museum in Drogheda.

I left the museum and climbed to the top of the grassy mound on which stands a round Martello-type tower, built about 1808. According to legend, the mound is the burial place of Amergin, poet and magician to the Milesians when they first landed in Ireland. The Normans fortified it in the twelfth century, and when Cromwell stormed Drogheda in 1649 the fort put up a determined resistance under the command of the governor of the town, Sir Arthur Aston, who was killed in the struggle. There is a fine view from this height over the surrounding countryside and it is easy to see why it was selected as a commanding strong point. The Republican forces occupied it in 1922 and were dislodged only when the Free State Army shelled it, doing considerable damage in the process.

From here it is a short walk to Mary Street, to see an extensive length of the old wall of the town at the rear of the churchyard of St. Mary's Protestant church, directly opposite the path leading from the front gate. Here Cromwell's cannon, mounted on the heights opposite, made the breach in the walls which enabled him to enter the town in September 1649. Looking across at the great mound surmounted by the fort, one wonders that it has not yet been excavated. It is true that it is only in the last twenty years or so that the great cemetery at Newgrange has been thoroughly investigated by archaeologists, and much work remains to be carried out there. One appreciates that archaeologists prefer to devote their limited time and resources to sites which are almost certain to yield worthwhile results and provide further knowledge of our Stone Age ancestors, but it must be acknowledged that the Boyne Valley monuments have received their due meed of attention. The great cairn on the top of Knockrea in County Sligo remains unexplored, for example. This is the legendary grave of the tempestuous Queen Maeve of Connacht, dominant figure in the *Táin Bó Cuailgne*. Millmount must wait its turn.

CHAPTER 8

Monasterboice - Mellifont - Baltray - Termonfechin -
Mornington

A pleasant church and with the linen altar-cloth,
a dwelling for God from Heaven:
Then, shining candles above the pure white Scriptures.
'Hermit's Song', trans. Kuno Meyer

Leaving Drogheda, I motored north on the Dunleer road and after five miles turned left on to a by-road and headed for Monasterboice Abbey. There were several more turns before I reached it, but signposts were plentiful and the round tower was plainly visible as I drew near. It was a grey misty day in February so I was the only visitor, and could stand and view Muiredach's Cross alone in the silence of the graveyard. How well it deserves its renown as one of the finest high crosses in the country. It stands seventeen feet eight inches high and the shaft and head are carved from one block of sandstone. Its massive and imposing proportions dwarf the surrounding tombstones. An inscription on the base asks for a prayer for Muiredach, 'by whom was made this cross'. Monasterboice was ruled by two abbots of that name; one died in the eighth century and the other, to whom the cross is generally attributed, in A.D. 923. So it has stood here for over a thousand years.

It is a scriptural cross, that is, the carvings depict scenes from the scriptures; the sculptor added decorative panels with interlacing motifs, vine scrolls and animals. The first panel at the bottom of the east face of the shaft shows Adam and Eve with the apple and the serpent, and Cain killing Abel. Above this is shown David with his sling and Goliath sinking to his knees. On the crossing, Christ appears in glory with the saved souls on one side of him and the damned on the other. Below him St.

Michael weighs the soul of the dead, with Satan trying to upset the balance. The panels on the west side have only three figures in each and show the Arrest of Christ, 'Doubting Thomas', Christ with St. Peter and St. Paul and the Crucifixion. The identification of Doubting Thomas is itself a subject of some doubt.

But a description of the scenes represented cannot convey the impact of these carvings. The bold relief employed enabled the sculptor, the Master of Monasterboice, to give the figures individuality in gesture and stance. The details of dress and accoutrements add authenticity to the representations; the soldiers carry swords and are dressed in baggy breeches, the priests or monks wear long robes and hold croziers or books. Abel, wearing a tunic, averts his head from the cleaver being brandished at him by a bearded Cain. It is not fanciful to see a look of sorrow and resignation on the victim's face, while around Cain there is an aura of menace. On the north side of the base, a pair of squatting figures pull each other's beards, taken by one commentator to be a symbol of lust. The Master seems to have revelled in the freedom afforded him by the larger space across the arms. The east side shows in the centre the Last Judgement, with Christ in Majesty carrying a cross and a flowering rod; at his left the Archangel Gabriel sounds his trumpet to summon the dead to rise. Across the arm, on Christ's left, the damned are being driven by Satan wielding a three-pronged fork, while an assistant devil launches a vicious kick to speed them on their way. At Christ's right, David with his harp leads the blessed in songs of praise. Between Satan and his assistant sits a remarkable splay-legged figure with arms folded across its chest. This figure is said to symbolise a grave sin, perhaps lust.

A few yards away stands the West or Tall Cross, ascribed to a later date than Muiredach's. It is aptly named, as it is almost twenty-three feet high and is the tallest in Ireland. The shaft has suffered considerably from weathering, especially at its base, but the cross head remains in remarkably good condition. This cross also shows scenes from the scriptures, and includes a unique carving of Christ walking on the water and saving

Muiredach's Cross at Monasterboice. This is one of the finest high crosses in Ireland. An inscription on the base asks for a prayer for Muiredach 'by whom was made this cross'.

Peter from drowning. On the right arm of the crosshead, Saints Peter and Paul stand one behind the other, pointing a crook-headed staff at a figure falling on its head. This has been ident-ified as 'The Fall of Simon Magus', which is a story handed down in tradition and not found in the scriptures. Simon Magus was a magician who boasted that he could fly through the air, but the combined prayers of the saints brought him crashing to his death before a large crowd. The scene can be regarded as a sym-bol of the triumph of the Church over heresy. Fortunately, both these unusual carvings are on the head of the cross and remain

Monasterboice, one of the tallest
round towers in Ireland.

clear and distinct. There is another cross in the north-east corner of the graveyard. It is much smaller than the other two, being only ten feet high, and only the head and upper part of the shaft belong to the original, the rest of the shaft being a replacement. The ornamentation consists only of a Crucifixion in the centre of the head on one side and a design of spirals on the other. Beside it there is a decorated sun dial, clearly marked off for the hours of 9 a.m., noon and 3 p.m., the canonical hours of tierce, sext and nones. The metal gnomon to direct the shadow on the marks has long since disappeared.

The round tower stands guard over the remains of two chur-

Above: Shaft panel, Monasterboice. This panel is carved on the shaft of Muiredach's Cross in a pattern of eight human figures, the knots being made out of their limbs, hair and beards.

Left: Sundial, Monasterboice. This sundial was used to fix the canonical hours of tierce, sext and nones, that is, 9 a.m., noon and 3 p.m. Such sundials were common on monastic sites in Ireland.

ches of no great interest. The tower is ninety-one feet high and has lost its top storey. It was burnt in 1097 and with it the monastic library and other treasures stored there. For many years the purpose for which round towers were built was the subject of acrimonious debate among scholars and antiquarians. They were variously described as Phoenician fire temples, minarets, phallic symbols and tombs. To George Petrie (1790-1866), goes the honour of settling the question in his famous essay read to the Royal Irish Academy and published in 1845. He showed that the towers were Christian ecclesiastical buildings, erected for use as belfries, watch-towers and keeps, and these findings are now generally accepted. There are still about eighty of these tall, slender towers surviving among the ruins of early monasteries. The present-day traveller making his way, as I did, along winding by-roads in search of antiquities is cheered and assured that he has taken the right turning when he sees the graceful shape of a round tower rising in the near distance. There is a fellow feeling for the pilgrim in medieval Ireland, trudging the weary miles to sit at the feet of Finian or Flann, whose heart lifts at the sound of a hand bell ringing out from the top of the monastery tower.

Monasterboice was founded by a saint called Buite who died in A.D. 521. Little is known about him or about the subsequent history of the foundation, probably because of the loss of the library in the burning of the tower in 1097. It seems that the monastery had a house for monks and another for nuns and that the nuns were lodged at some distance from the monks' quarters 'lest harm be done to the fair name of the religious'. Monasterboice gained a high reputation as a centre of learning; its most distinguished teacher was Flann, who died in 1056 and who was noted in the *Annals of the Four Masters* as 'the outstanding master of Ireland in wisdom, literature, history, poetry and science'. After the foundation of Mellifont by the Cistercians in 1142 on a site only a few miles away, the fame of Monasterboice declined and it seems that its patronage and support was drawn away from it by the new monastery.

The site is well looked after by the Board of Works. Mrs.

Panel from Muiredach's Cross at Monasterboice showing the Arrest of Christ. This cross is classed as a scriptural cross as the carvings depict scenes from Old and New Testaments.

Crilly, who lives beside it, told me that a team from FAS would be coming in the summer to tidy up the graveyard. Some elm trees near the tower have the Dutch disease and will be felled. There is anxiety that vandals might damage the crosses and a suggestion that they might be removed to a museum for safe keeping. The anxiety is understandable but it would be a great pity to take them away from their centuries-old environment which adds so much to the pleasure of viewing them.

At Mrs. Crilly's house I met local historian Kenneth Mac-Gowan, who told me I should look at the headstone over the grave of Eamonn Penthony. The story goes that Eamonn wanted to make sure that he would be remembered properly, so he wrote the inscription himself in Irish and had the headstone carved and put in place over the grave when he was in his sixties, with a space left for the date of his death. I went back into the graveyard and found the stone near the tower. The lettering is in the Gaelic script and describes Eamonn as a patriot and lifelong member of the Gaelic League who worked zealously for the advancement of the Irish language. He was born in 1877 and lived to be ninety-four, so that the headstone was in place for thirty years waiting for the final inscription, the date of his death in 1971. Kenneth also told me about Michael Derby, who lived in the house now occupied by the Crillys and was caretaker of the abbey until his death a few years ago. He was very proud of his charge and had learnt off by heart Professor R.A.S. Macalister's description of the monuments, which he would recite to visitors as he conducted them around the site.

As I left to take the road south-west to Mellifont I took a last look at the round tower:

> The sweet little bell
> That is struck in the windy night,
> Sooner would I tryst with that
> Than tryst with a lustful woman.
> (*Trans. David Greene*)

This is a countryside of rolling hills, dotted with clumps of trees. Thick hedgerows divide the wide green fields, providing shelter for wildlife — the song thrush, blackbirds, wrens, hedge-hogs and other small animals. There is a feeling of permanence about this landscape intensified by the stillness, the lack of traffic, a feeling that the hand of man has done little to disturb or change it for centuries. And so I journeyed on to Mellifont, — An Mhainistir Mhór, 'The Great Monastery' — tucked away in a small secluded valley on the banks of the Mattock river, a tributary of the Boyne, which it joins at Oldbridge. Again there were twists and turns in the road, and crossroads, but all are well signposted with The Boyne Drive, Slí na Bóinne, marked by special green signs. As I stopped at one crossroads to get my bearings a car halted beside me and a deep Meath voice asked if I was lost.

'No, just making out the different roads. The signposts are very good.'

'They are, but sometimes jokers come and turn them round. Good luck.' And with a laugh and a wave he was on his way.

The site of Mellifont, the first Cistercian monastery in Ireland, was specially chosen by its founder St. Malachy for its resemblance to the site of Clairvaux, the mother house in France, presided over by his friend St. Bernard. Donogh O'Carroll, Prince of Oriel, granted the lands and gave a generous endowment. St. Bernard sent a band of monks from Clairvaux to help in the foundation, and an experienced architect named Robert to assist in building the church. The monastery was founded in 1142 and consecrated with great pomp in 1157 in a ceremony attended by kings and prelates. Daughter abbeys quickly sprang up, including that at Bective which we saw earlier on. As one approaches Mellifont down a narrow side road, it becomes clear how well St. Malachy heeded the advice of St. Bernard to choose a site 'apart from the commotions of the world'. At the entrance to the abbey, there is a flat stone on the perimeter wall and the Board of Works have placed on it a very informative plan, similar to that at Bective, showing the dates and names of the different buildings — refectory, infirmary, chapter house and lavabo. Originally there was a fountain in the lavabo where the monks washed before going into the adjoining refectory. The chapter house is a fine vaulted building with a groined roof; a quantity of carved stones, tiles and other fragments of the ancient buildings are stored there.

Devorgilla, the estranged wife of Ua Ruairc, Prince of Breifne, is said to have passed her last years here in penance and good works and to have been buried under the sedilia, the recessed seats beside the altar. She was abducted by Diarmuid MacMurrough, King of Leinster, in a raid on Breifne in 1152; some of the annalists record that the lady went not unwillingly. She returned to Ua Ruairc a year later and shortly after retired to Mellifont, dying there in 1193 at the age of eighty-five. This was the same Diarmuid MacMurrough who first brought the Normans to Ireland and earned the name Diarmuid na nGall, 'Diarmuid of the Foreigners'.

After spending a quiet, meditative hour pacing the gravelled walks between the ruined buildings, I took the road to Collon to meet Father Colmcille at New Mellifont. The road rises up the Hill of Collon above the village, giving a fine view on all sides. From higher up on Mount Oriel, it is possible to see the Mourne mountains away north and the Wicklow hills to the south. When the Cistercians returned to the district in 1939, they settled in Oriel Temple, a fine house built by John Foster, last Speaker of the Irish House of Commons, who was born in Collon House in the village, about a mile from Oriel Temple. Collon is pronounced 'Cullen' and means 'hazel nut'.

I enquired from Father Colmcille about Count Tolstoy, grandnephew of the great Russian novelist, Count Leo Tolstoy, who had lived in Collon during the war years, and had given tuition in Russian to a number of students, including Conor Cruise O'Brien, Máire Mhac an tSaoi and Eoin MacWhite who were then attached to the Department of External Affairs, and their friend Art O'Beolain, then as now a devoted Russophile. Yes, he had known Tolstoy and also another Russian called Nikolai Couriss, who with his wife Tanya had joined with Count Tolstoy in the teaching enterprise. Couriss was an ex-officer in the Cossacks, who had fled into exile from the post-Tsarist regime after the revolution of 1917. He eventually settled in

Lavabo at Mellifont Abbey. St. Malachy founded the first Irish Cistercian monastery at Mellifont in 1142. The lavabo, a remarkable octagonal two-storeyed building, held a fountain at which the monks washed their hands before going to eat in the nearby refectory.

Collon, where he lived in the old courthouse. During World War II he set up a small charcoal-burning enterprise. Older readers may recall the unwieldy apparatus mounted on the rear end of motor cars, with charcoal-generated gas supplying the motive power. Later, after his wife and child had died, the ex-Cossack determined to enter the priesthood. From the Cistercians in New Mellifont he borrowed theological works, studied assiduously and was ordained priest in the Russian Orthodox Church, going to the United States for the purpose. On his return he was appointed parish priest for all the Russian and Greek Orthodox Catholics in Ireland. He removed to Dublin and died there some years ago.

On the subject of learning Russian, Father Colmcille reminded me that the late Professor Michael O'Brien of the Dublin Institute of Advanced Studies (brother of the late Tommy O'Brien of RTE's 'Your Choice and Mine') prepared dictionaries of Russian-English and English-Russian, and that these dictionaries are officially supplied to Russian embassies and consulates in English-speaking countries and to their British counterparts in Soviet Russia, a tribute to Irish scholarship that should be better known. His feat is all the more remarkable when it is remembered that he did this work when he was a student in Germany. Short of money, like students everywhere, he sold the copyright for a miserably small sum, losing valuable royalties that are still being paid to the subsequent owner.

From Collon I motored back to Drogheda and then took the coast road to Baltray and Termonfechin. Passing by the Boyne Viaduct, I remembered the manoeuvre watched so often by the townspeople as the *Mellifont* or *Colleen Bawn* swung around in the river and berthed with bow facing seawards, ready for the outward passage. These ships were almost as long as the full width of the river at full tide, and it required skill and a nice touch with both helm and engines to carry out the manoeuvre successfully. The ship would be steered almost, but not quite, into the soft mud on the Meath side just above the Viaduct, and as the flood tide swung her stern around, it was slow astern on the engines and she would back gently across to her berth. It was only too easy to get her bow stuck in the mud and then to go astern too hard in the effort to extricate the vessel, which would tend to come back across to the quay wall at terrifying speed. Dockside loafers and longshoremen were connoisseurs of this free spectacle, and the misfortunes of one captain were retailed over many a pint. On that well-remembered occasion, he had got his ship stuck in the mud, there was great shouting of advice from the quayside, a boat put off and took a line ashore with a hawser attached. Willing hands hauled it to a bollard, dropped the loop over and the shout went up, 'Heave away!' But the ship's crew hove in too enthusiastically on the capstan, the hawser tightened, sprang out of the water and the ship came out of the mud like a cork out of a bottle. The pandemonium was complete. Majestically the vessel bore down on the quay and her high counter swept away ten yards of railing and a watchman's hut. A heaving line was thrown from her bows but fell short. Another boat put off, retrieved the line and got it ashore. It is far from easy to control several thousand tons of ship on a flood tide in a narrow channel, and a full hour of drama followed before the vessel was safely moored alongside, with her captain and the harbour master gloomily contemplating the damage to ship and quayworks.

If a vessel failed to catch the tide and met the ebb sweeping out under the Viaduct, she might be just in time to berth but too late to swing, and she would have to lie alongside the quay with her bow facing upriver. Hence the origin of the local saying in answer to the question 'Were you in time?', 'Only just, I got there bow up.' Captain William Hanrahan, the present harbour master, tells me that ships above ninety metres in length are not allowed into the port of Drogheda as they could not be swung with safety. A pilot must be taken on board to navigate ships up the river from the bar; they are licensed and employed by the Harbour Commissioners and work on a rota. I remembered a tragedy of the 1920s, before the introduction of the rota system, when it was the practice that the pilotage went to the first pilot to stand on the deck of an incoming ship. Two pilots were racing for a ship on a wild October day, with a high sea running. 'Lar' Garvey was first alongside. 'Jump, Lar, jump,' his crew shouted. Lar sprang for the rail, missed his handhold and fell into the sea between the side of the ship and his boat. His seaboots and heavy oilskins pulled him down. Public shock at this drowning led the Harbour Commissioners to take a hard look at the traditional pilotage practice and to change it to the present rota system. In the museum in Millmount there is a certificate issued to Pilot Nicholas Boylan of Baltray alongside his silver medal, a badge and sign of office which he wore round his neck and which he had to show to the master of the vessel before he would be taken on. The medal is engraved with his name, his age (30), height (5ft 9 1/2 inches) and the date (1810).

The road to Baltray — Baile an Trá, 'The Town of the Strand' — runs alongside the Boyne and is separated from it for most of the way by a salt marsh, haunt of gulls, oystercatchers, sanderlings, redshanks and many other waders. Part of this area has been designated a wildlife sanctuary by the Forest and Wildlife Service. Many seafarers and pilots came from the village in the days when ships required large crews. I drove on to Termonfechin to visit An Grianán, 'The Sunny Bower', the residential college run by the Irish Countrywomen's Association, Bantract na hEireann. Formerly the home of the Lentaigne family, the fine building was acquired by the I.C.A. in 1954 with a grant from the Kellogg Foundation of America. It is set in pleasant parkland of about eighty acres and approached by an avenue of elm trees, some 150 years old. The courses in adult education have proved very successful, and a horticultural college for women was initiated in the 1960s. Conferences, seminars, lectures, concerts and plays are included in the activities. Mr. James Creed, Director of An Grianán, kindly showed me round; the friendly and cheerful atmosphere could be felt at once. A visit to An Grianán dispels gloomy thoughts about the prospects of the country. It is well named — The Sunny Bower — to lift one's spirits and give hope for the future.

Termonfechin is the anglicised form of the Irish Tearmonn Fechin, 'St. Fechin's Sanctuary Land'. St. Fechin founded a monastery here in the seventh century. In the graveyard of the Protestant church there is a scriptural high cross, with a carving of the Crucifixion and of Christ in Glory. Built into the porch of the church is a stone bearing the inscription *Oroit do ultan et do Dubthach do Rigne in Caissel*, 'a prayer for Ultan and Dubthach who made this stone fort'. Close by is Termonfechin Castle, a fifteenth- or sixteenth-century tower house of three storeys in good condition. The primates of Armagh, who lived in Drogheda from the fourteenth century down to 1835, had a summer residence in Termonfechin; Oliver Plunkett and James Ussher are among the archbishops said to have lived there. The Ecclesiastical Courts of Armagh were held in Drogheda, but when the primate was in residence in Termonfechin the court moved there with him. A manuscript in Armagh Public Library records a public penance inflicted on a gentleman of Termonfechin who had been convicted of perjury. He had 'to walk around the cemetery clothed in white linen on six different Sundays, and to fast on bread and water for three days.' These two quiet villages make an ideal weekend retreat for town or city dwellers, offering a fine, safe beach, an eighteen-hole golf course, pleasant walks and abundant bird life on shore, salt marsh and in secluded lanes.

Baltray has its counterpart on the south side of the estuary, a village called Mornington. Approaching it from Drogheda, you get a splendid view of Beaulieu House, set on a hill rising over the far bank, surrounded by trees and with a fine lawn sloping down towards the Boyne. From the time of the Norman invasion the estate belonged to the Plunketts, who were related to the great noble families of the Pale, headed by Lords Fingal, Dunsany and Louth. St. Oliver Plunkett was of that family. Under the Cromwellian regime, the lands were acquired by Sir Henry Tichborne, who in 1660 built himself this beautiful brick mansion, the earliest example still existing in Ireland of an unfortified gentleman's residence. It is the finest and best preserved Irish country house of the second half of the seventeenth century, and is still occupied by descendants of the original owners.

There was great rivalry years ago between the two villages, and when a Mornington man married a Baltray girl he was asked why he married a foreigner! There are two curious structures by the shore, the Maiden Tower and the Lady's Finger. The tower is about eighty feet high and is used as a beacon to guide ships entering the Boyne estuary; a winding stairway inside gives access to the top of the tower. Sir William Wilde writes that not many years before he published his book in 1849, a poor half-witted female recluse took up her abode on the top of the tower, and was, like the hermits of old, 'supplied with every necessary by the surrounding peasantry'. The tower dates from Elizabethan days and hence, it was said, the name 'Maiden', after the queen. Other accounts say that it was built by a maiden to watch out for the return of her betrothed from an expedition abroad. If he had been successful, he was to hoist a white flag, if not, a black one. The lover on his return, seeing the tower for the first time and mistaking it for that of an invading enemy, hoisted a black flag. The maiden in a fit of despair, flung herself from the tower and was killed. These stories aside, it is so well placed to act as a beacon and watch tower that it is virtually certain it was built for these purposes. The so-called 'Lady's Finger' is more puzzling; a solid pillar forty feet high, it does not at all resemble a finger, and may be a phallic symbol of date unknown.

South from Mornington are the seaside villages of Bettystown and Laytown, with fine, safe strands. Meath and Louth are 'horsy' counties and the Strand Races are the best of fun.

On 24 August 1850, a child walking near Bettystown shore picked up a bright metallic object at the foot of a cliff from which a large piece had recently fallen. She brought it home to her mother, a poor woman, who sold it to a watchmaker in Drogheda. From him it passed to a Dublin jeweller, who recognised it as a brooch of rare quality which must have belonged to a prince or king and called it the Tara Brooch. From him it passed to the National Museum. It has been dated to the eighth century, and is an example of the superb craftsmanship of the Irish metalworkers of that time.

CHAPTER 9

Pilgrim's Way

And took my pleasant pilgrimage,
To see the sweet Boyne water.
Old ballad

Like all pilgrims, I want to return again and again to the paths and byways that gave so much pleasure on the way, to see again the enchanting weir at Carrickdexter, and sit for a while in the quiet of Monasterboice beside the Cross of Muiredach. There are so many other places yet to visit: the village of Summerhill; Duleek, where the Jacobite army halted in their retreat from the Boyne, and where Dame Jennett Dowdall 'builded' a cross (which still stands) to the memory of her husband who died in 1509: Dunsany, seat of a branch of the Plunkett family, where the fifteenth-century church holds one of the finest medieval fonts in Ireland, and where the eighteenth Baron, Edward John Moreton Drax (1878-1957), was soldier, big-game hunter, chess champion, prolific author and friend of his Meath neighbours, Francis Ledwidge and Mary Lavin; Rathcarne and Gibbstown, near Athboy, where, between 1935 and 1940, 122 families from the Gaeltacht were settled on new holdings carved out from fertile Meath estates — a bold experiment, today it is still a Gaeltacht, officially recognised as such. This would have pleased that noted worker in the language revival, Father Eugene O'Growney (1861-1899), Professor of Irish at Maynooth and author of *Simple Lessons in Irish*, who was born and brought up at Ballyfallon, only a mile and a half from Athboy.

Places and people: Tom Cassidy of Knowth, nearing ninety years of age, six feet two and straight as a lance, spoke to me of the young Francis Ledwidge, whom he knew as an unworldly, dreamy young man. He told me of being sent into Drogheda before World War I with a horse and cart, to buy coal at seven shillings and sixpence (37 1/2 pence) a ton. The coal had been brought from Whitehaven in a small sailing ship, the *Glad Tidings*, owned by the Whitehead family, and when they had sold their cargo, the crew of three brothers with their father as skipper set sail again across the Irish Sea for another load. A gale sprang up and *Glad Tidings* was never heard of again, lost with all hands. As he spoke, I remembered hearing that story myself from old people, who said sadly that the crew were 'fine young lads, all of them, but the sea knows no pity.'

Talk of olden days brought back memories of summer days in Baltray long ago, helping with the hay, riding on a low float behind the plodding horse, watching the men winching the haystack on to it and sitting with back to the stack or trotting alongside to the farmyard. And that lost pleasure, bowling along a country lane in a smart trap with a lively pony between the shafts, and being allowed to take the reins for a mile or two.

Conor Brennan of Beauparc, now over seventy, has spent his working life as gardener with the 'big houses' along the banks of the Boyne. He pointed out to me the hill where copper was mined down to 1913 and where Ledwidge worked for a while and organised a strike to improve conditions. Like so many of the local people I met, Conor Brennan is proud of his heritage and knowledgeable about places and people. The name 'Beauparc' he regards as an alien intrusion and he calls his own house 'The Furze' to remind neighbours and visitors of the old name of the district. He remembers when you would see twenty or thirty rods fishing the Boyne above Slane. As we talked, I was reminded that this was the Pale of former days, and vestiges of the connection with England still remain. 'Two ministers of the Crown had strong attachments round here,' he said. 'There was Lord Brabazon of Tara, the pioneer airman, and Brendan Bracken, who came often to stay with the Laffans not far from here.' He laughed, 'And you'll find a field down the road and it's still called "Cromwell's meadow".' He regrets the way old buildings were demolished. 'There was a windmill over there,' he

Beaulieu House, near Drogheda, was built by Sir Henry Tichbourne in 1660. It is the earliest example of an unfortified gentleman's house now existing in Ireland and is still occupied by descendants of the original owners.
A beautiful house on a beautiful site.
(Detail below.)

points, 'but they pulled it down and used the stones for walls.
Now, why wouldn't they have left it and it would be an addition
to that hill? And when I was working on the Lambart estate
and they'd talk about concrete for a wall or path, I'd say, haven't
we got great stone that'll wear better than concrete and look
better, too. When you go down the road,' he said, 'stop at the
bridge over the railway by the football field. That's the Skew
Bridge, they had to build it skew-ways because the road takes
a sharp bend there. The people from the Railway Society come
here regularly and they do admire the stonework and how the
mason cut the arch stones and fitted them for the skew.'

There is the story of the Boyne Navigation, incorporating
both river and canal. Work on it began as far back as 1748. In
1790 the Boyne Navigation Company was established by Act of
Parliament and by 1800 the waterway from Drogheda to Navan
had been completed. The River Boyne Company took over then.
There were twelve boats from forty to sixty tons burthen plying
on the river and canal, carrying flour, oats, barley, yarn and
linen downstream and coal, culm, timber, iron and salt up-
stream. The extension of the railway from Drogheda to Navan
in 1850 was an ominous development, but the Navigation
struggled on. In the early years of this century it enjoyed a
period of prosperity as a tourist attraction. A steam launch
made regular trips from Oldbridge to Slane and Beauparc. The
photographs from the Lawrence Collection show why the local
guide-book told visitors that 'this part of the river cannot be
surpassed for fine views and foliage'.

James McCann, Nationalist M.P., and banker, who came
from Drogheda, leased the Navigation for seven years from
1902 but his sudden death in 1904 was a severe blow to the
enterprise. Business fell off and the company went into liquid-
ation in 1913. For the second time, a local businessman came
to the rescue. John Spicer, a son-in-law of James McCann and
head of the firm that owned the Boyne and Blackwater flour
mills in Navan, took over the undertaking in 1915. But official
support and funds were lacking, business continued to decline
and by 1925 the canal was virtually abandoned and fell rapidly

into decay for want of maintenance. In 1969 John Spicer generously donated the entire property to An Taisce as a public amenity, so that the Boyne Walk could still be enjoyed.

The canal is not continuous and boats must change from canal to river and back again in their passage. As well, the canal runs sometimes on the north bank of the river and sometimes on the south bank. When goods were carried by barges drawn by horses and the barges came to a part where the canal moved to the other side, the horse stepped on to the barge and was conveyed to the towpath on the far side, where he was led ashore and resumed his ordinary labours.

At Oldbridge and Slane I had seen men working on short stretches of the canal, a hopeful sign that, in time, it will be open and navigable again all the way to Navan, a most pleasing prospect; and meanwhile the Boyne Walk remains, thanks to John Spicer and An Taisce. There is hopeful news, too, about the Boyne itself. The Department of Fisheries and the Board of Works are planning a programme of rehabilitation to remedy the despoliation caused by the recent large-scale arterial drainage. Gravel will be relaid for spawning beds, large rocks placed to make runs and shelters for trout, weirs and small piers built in suitable locations. And the river bank, which was stripped of many fine trees impeding the path of the huge drainage machines, will be replanted. Furthermore, Meath County Council in its County Development Plan gave official recognition to the 'immense recreational and cultural values of the Boyne Valley' and pledges itself to safeguard its natural beauty and environment from undesirable and incompatible development and to enhance its amenity potential.

Five thousand years ago Neolithic man settled in this valley and raised great monuments. Kings reigned at Tara until St. Patrick brought the message of Christianity. Celtic Ireland adapted its ways to the new belief; monasteries, learning and art flourished. Norman families built fine mansions on wooded heights — Nangles at Ardsallagh, D'Arcys at Plattin, Dowdalls at Athlumney and Flemings at Slane. History came full circle when Irish-speaking descendants of those whom Cromwell had

Dancing on the pier at Clogher Head. In the thirties on fine summer evenings the people from neighbouring towns and villages cycled, walked or motored to the seaside. Here they dance on Clogher Head pier, evoking a past that seems much further away than fifty years.

banished 'to Hell or to Connacht' returned to settle on these rich Meath lands.

The foregoing pages are no more than an introduction to the long and varied history of the Boyne Valley, and a celebration of its present beauties and past glories. The list of books for further reading includes detailed guidebooks to encourage exploration. Above all, visits should not be rushed and hurried; allow for time to walk and time to stand and stare.

Go n-eirí an bóthar libh.

Suggested Further Reading

Brennan, Martin, *The Boyne Valley Vision* (Dublin 1980)

De Paor, Liam and Máire, *Early Christian Ireland* (London 1958)

Ellison, Cyril, *The waters of the Boyne and Blackwater*, (Dublin 1983)

Eogan, George, *Knowth and the Passage Tombs of Ireland*, (London 1986)

Garner, William, *Drogheda Architectural Heritage*, (Dublin 1986)

Harbison, Peter, *Guide to the National Monuments of Ireland*, (Dublin 1970)

Hickey, Elizabeth, *I Send My Love Along the Boyne*, (Dublin 1966)

Killanin and Duignan, *Shell Guide to Ireland*, (London 1962)

D'Alton, John, *History of Drogheda*, (Dublin 1844)

Mitchell, Frank, *Shell Guide to Irish Landscape*, (Dublin 1986)

O'Callaghan, John Cornelius, *The Green Book*, (Dublin 1845)

Roe, Helen, *Monasterboice and its Monuments*, (Dundalk 1981)

Story, George, *An Impartial History of the Wars of Ireland*, (London 1693)

Trench, C.E.F., *Slane*, (An Taisce Meath Association 1987 Slane Co. Meath)

Weir, Anthony, *Early Ireland, A Field Guide*, (Belfast 1980)

Wilde, Sir William, *The Beauties of the Boyne and Blackwater*, (Dublin 1849)

Journals of Co. Louth Archaeology Society, Old Drogheda Society
and Ríocht na Mí

Acknowledgements

The author and publisher wish to thank the following for the illustrations appearing in this book: the National Library of Ireland for pp 2, 8, 53 bottom, 71, 73, 75, 104, 107, 129, 131 bottom; the Commissioners of Public Works for pp 3, 4, 5, 6, 30, 49, 53 top, 58, 63, 78 top and bottom, 82 bottom, 83, 87, 89, 91, 93, 121, 141, 145, 149; the National Gallery of Ireland for pp 25 bottom left and right, 110, 112, 131 top, 157; Bord Failte for pp 25 top, 33, 65 bottom, 115; D. Newman Johnson for drawing p.20 top; Dr Peter Harbison for photograph p.46; Dundalgan Press for p. 20 bottom; photographs p.160 by Maurice Curtin and p.137 by Albert Eskerod are reproduced by kind permission of the Head of the Department of Folklore, University College Dublin.

For the W.B.Yeats extract A.P.Watt, London, and Macmillan Publishing Inc., New York

Engravings used throughout the book are from William Wilde's *Boyne and Blackwater*. The artist and antiquary William Wakeman drew the fine illustrations for Wilde's book.Whilst they may not have the detail and accuracy of modern archaeological work, these century-old sketches capture, with great sympathy, the beauty and mystery of these places.

Index